A GIRL'S GUIDE TO A GUY'S WORLD

JENNIFER BABBIT
&
SAMANTHA BANK

LONGSTREET PRESS
Atlanta

Published by
LONGSTREET PRESS, INC.
2140 Newmarket Parkway
Suite 122
Marietta, GA 30067

Printed in the United States of America

1st printing 2001

Library of Congress Catalog Card Number: 00-111981

ISBN: 1-56352-649-2

Jacket design by Holly Peyer, Brett Schindler, and Chris Bingaman
Book design by Burtch Bennett Hunter
Photographs by Arie Goldman

TO OUR FAMILIES

Table of Contents

A GIRL'S GUIDE
TO A
GUY'S WORLD

Introduction

Sam called me in April complaining about all the problems she was having with her new apartment and how she couldn't seem to fix any of these problems by herself. For even the smallest of situations, she had to call her brother, her father, or her boyfriend to ask for help. "Why do they know how to do all these things and we don't?" she asked in frustration. "We should write a book for all the women in this world who are in the same situation. Somewhere along the way, we missed the basic 'how-to' instruction session that men have mastered." As we began surveying our friends, we were astounded both by the number of women in the same boat as us and by the number of women who wanted to get off that boat! After years of collaboration on various projects, Sam and I simply decided, "O.K., let's do it! Let's teach ourselves those basics that most men know and then share our findings with other women."

Unfortunately, women often use the excuse that due to gender-related social conditions, we are incapable of doing certain things that men can do. But let's face it, in an age when women are much more independent, living alone, and getting married later in life, it's time to stop with the excuses. When given the proper instruction, women are equally capable of performing "masculine" tasks. In fact, I bet we can probably tackle this "manly" stuff more efficiently and with much more sass and class. (Don't share this opinion with your guy friends – we don't want to trigger some sort of macho-hormonal imbalance.)

Enough excuses! Ladies, this is a book about those things typically considered "guy stuff." Its valuable lessons will enable you to rely on your own ingenuity and intellect. As a result, you will no longer need to call your brother, father, or boyfriend with desperate pleas for help. We hope that by reading this book and using it as a reference, you'll be able to relate to and impress your male counterparts with witty conversational tidbits. Furthermore, this girly guide provides great "how-to" segments that will make you feel more secure as an independent woman ... and even save you some extra cash. Keep this *Girl's Guide* handy. You never know when its helpful hints and easy-to-follow how-tos will prove useful.

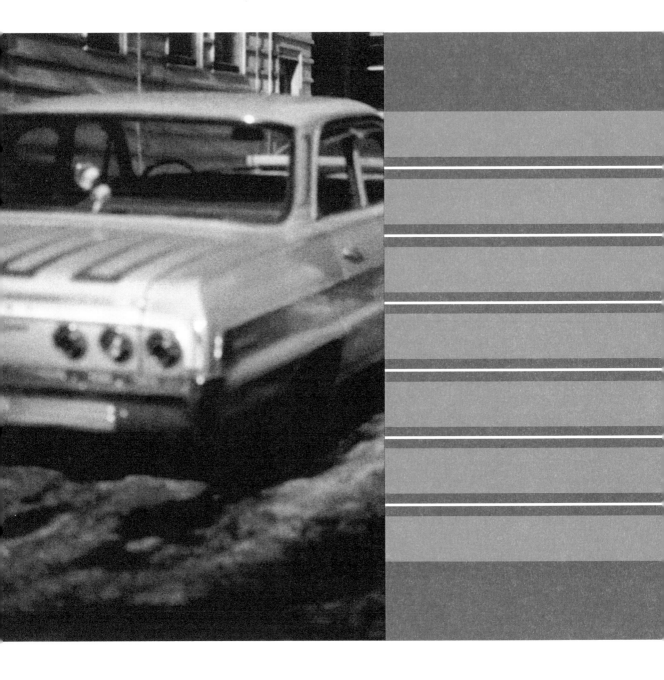

THE CAR

Isn't it mind-boggling how a guy can ramble off ridiculous facts and statistics for virtually any and every type of car? Facts ranging from its make and model to its rims and acceleration speed are all at his fingertips, yet ask him when his mother's birthday is and he'll be dumbfounded. While we don't know the real reason for this male phenomenon, we can help you understand some of the car world's essential info. As a result, you'll be able to wow your male buddies with your newfound knowledge.

Jenn and I got into our first car accident together in the middle of a busy Atlanta shopping center. As soon as Jenn hit the other car, she immediately burst into tears. She was too shaken to call for help, so I dialed up my father to deliver the news and seek his guidance. As if calling dear old Dad wasn't embarrassing enough, all our friends gathered around Jenn's car and dished out unsolicited advice. When you do encounter the trauma of a car accident – be it a minor fender bender or a more serious situation, the most important thing to remember is to immediately call the police. No matter how minimal the damage, it is imperative that the police file a report for your insurance company and solidify the facts surrounding the accident. Be sure to have your driver's license and insurance information ready once the police arrive at the scene.

If by some misfortune you happen to find yourself in a car catastrophe, or want to avoid one altogether, check out what we put together for you. The following chapter is full of useful tips and procedures to help you through some basic, but frequent, car emergencies.

VOCABULARY

Alternator: A generator that produces alternating current for powering the electrical equipment while the engine is running.

Diesel engine: An engine without a carburetor that uses diesel oil rather than gasoline.

Horsepower: The energy required to lift 550 pounds 1 foot in 1 second – in other words, the pulling power of the engine. This term is rooted in the horse-and-buggy tradition, which was a precursor to the automobile. The greater number of horses pulling the buggy, the faster the vehicle. The same concept holds true with today's automobiles. Small, compact cars or sedans are usually built with less horsepower than SUVs because they have less weight to pull.

Transmission: The gearbox that transmits power from the engine to the axle through various gear ratios.

Lug Nut: The large nuts that lock the wheel onto the car.

HISTORY OF THE AUTOMOBILE

In Latin, the word "auto" means self and the word "mobile" means movement, and in the old Celtic language, "car" means cart or wagon. In 1879, George Selden created and then patented the first-ever road machine. In 1895, the Duryea Brothers called their products "motor wag-ons," and were credit-ed with building the first internal combus-tion car. Henry Ford introduced his experi-mental car called the "Quadricyle" in 1896, and later went on to become one of the biggest car distributors of his time. The first popular car was the Oldsmobile; it had two seats, one cylinder, and a three horsepower engine.

Hubcap Recap

In 1917, the first heaters were installed in automobiles.

~

In 1925, Mr. Hertz started the first rental car company in the United States.

~

In 1931, sunvisors were first installed in the interior of cars.

~

And in 1959, seat belts were first installed in cars, beginning with the Volvo.

CHANGING A FLAT TIRE

When you're cruising down the road with your girlfriends feeling like *Thelma and Louise* badasses, there's nothing worse than a flat tire! If you have a cell phone, you could call AAA, but ladies, be prepared for a long wait. Or you could change the tire on your own. Don't panic – this is easy. We'll walk you through it.

Step 1: First things first: before you ever hit the road, check and make sure you have all the essential gear. You should find the items you're looking for under the rear of your trunk: a spare tire (doughnut or full size), a jack, and a lug wrench. (**Note – If you bought your car used, there is a good possibility some of this stuff could be missing and will need replacing.)

Step 2: O.K. When your drive is feeling anything but smooth, it's usually a good indication that you've got a flat. The first thing you need to do is find a safe location to pull over. Find a level area away from any traffic. It is better to pull over as soon as possible in order to do the least amount of damage to your tire and car. Once you have pulled over, remember to put on your hazards – especially at night.

Step 3: Pull out the tools (lug wrench, jack, jack handle, and spare) from your trunk and roll up your sleeves. First you will need to loosen the lug nuts. On some cars, the lug nuts are hidden by a cover or hubcap. If that's the case, then you can use the flat end of the lug wrench to pry it off. There is a slot on the edge of the plate to help you do this. After removing the hubcap, find the end of the wrench that fits correctly over the lug nuts. Turn the wrench counter-clockwise to loosen the lug nuts. This can be pretty difficult. The easiest thing to do is to use your body weight and actually bounce up and down on the wrench. (Finally those extra chocolates you ate will come in handy!) Be careful when you do this! Place your foot at the end of the wrench and hold onto the car for support. There are usually four or five lug nuts that will need loosening. After loosening the nuts you will raise the car. Some cars have an anti-theft device where one lug nut is a different size than the rest. If that is the case, use a special key (found in the trunk toolbox) to loosen it.

Step 4: You're now ready to jack up the car. In order to replace a flat tire, you need to raise that respective corner of the car. Using the jack handle that fits into the socket on the jack, you will raise the car through a swiveling or scissor-type motion. It sounds difficult, but it's really not that complicated. It is imperative that you place your jack in the correct spot. Your car manual should contain this information. Generally, the spot is about half a foot to a foot behind the front tire and the same distance in front of the rear tire. There should be some form of grooves, or even a slide, to fit the jack in. Once you've got the jack in the right spot, turn the handle so that the car rises off the ground. Remember, you have to fit a fully inflated tire onto the car – be sure to give it ample room.

World Record

According to *The Guiness Book of World Records 2001*, the United States is the country with the highest number of cars, with over 135 million. That amounts to one car for every two Americans. This figure doesn't even include trucks, campers and motorcycles. Japan is second with 44.6 million cars and in third place is Germany with 40.5 million.

Step 5: At this point, you will need to remove the already loosened lug nuts. Be sure not to lose them! Next, you want to grasp the tire and pull it straight out and off of the car. Keep your weight forward so that you don't lose your balance. Roll the tire to the side.

Step 6: Now it's time to put on the spare. Hold it up and try to line up the holes with the corresponding shafts. Put it on so that the wheel is seated correctly and can't be pushed any further in. Take the lug nuts and put them on with your hands. You can use the wrench to turn them slightly so that they all rest against the wheel. Don't tighten them until you lower the jack so that the tire just rests on the ground. When you tighten the lug nuts, begin with one and then do the nut on the opposite side. Do the remaining lug nuts in the same manner. If your car has five nuts, tighten every other one until they are all completed.

Step 7: You're almost ready to get back on the road. Pack up all your gear and put the flat tire in your car. Also be sure to return the jack and lug wrench to your toolbox. If you did have a hubcap, you can hold one edge in place and use the heel of your hand to bang on the opposite end. If you are using a spare, drive carefully and slowly. Generally the tire will have its maximum speed posted on its side. (Typically it's about 50 mph). Remember that since it is only a spare, you need to take your car to the shop ASAP to fix or replace it with a real tire.

CAR-BUYING TIPS

When my mother bought her first car, she went to the dealership all by herself, selected her car, and bought it on her own. She was so proud of herself for being so independent. When she got home, she called her best friend to share her excitement. Coincidentally, her friend had purchased the exact same car. To my mom's surprise, her best friend had gone to the dealership with her husband and bought the car for $1,000 less than my mom! My mother called the president of the car company and told him her story. The following week, she received a check from the president himself for $1,000. Way to go, Mom!

So that this kind of thing doesn't happen to you, here are some quick tips on buying a new car:

❀ It is usually cheaper for dealers to order a standard options package than specific custom settings, so it's a better deal to order the luxury package rather than a handful of select options.

❀ When the manufacturer of a car sells it to the dealer, the price usually includes extra benefits such as a car wash or a tank of gas. Be sure to ask your dealer about added benefits.

❀ Take advantage of the always-resourceful Internet when buying a new car and check out these great sites: autotrader.com, auto-bytel.com, vehix.com, or mileone.com.

❀ You can often find great deals during the month of December because dealer-ships are trying to clear out inventory to make room for the new year's edition. You might even get lucky and find a Christmas-time clearance sale. Also remember to go car shopping during the last weekend of the month. Certain dealerships have to meet a monthly quota. As a result, they are more likely to give you a deal in order to make the sale.

❀ It is in your best interest to bargain. Never take the first offer. In fact, decide on a set price that you are willing to spend. When stating your first bid, announce an amount lower than your set price. This allows for bargaining power.

❀ Be patient! Take your time and shop around. A car is a big investment and you want to put in the proper amount of time doing your research. Be a smart consumer.

Buying a new car in many ways can be a lot simpler than purchasing a used car. After months of excitement and careful consideration, my friend decided to pur-chase what she believed to be a great used car. The mileage was low and the price was reasonable. Three weeks after her pur-chase, she noticed a problem with her dri-ver's side door. She took the car to the mechanic and he informed her that the car had obviously been in quite an accident. Luckily she was able to return the car, but lost almost $2000 in the exchange. Don't let this happen to you! There are many things to check when purchasing a used car. Here are a few. . . .

❀ Ask the seller a few key questions: "Are you the first owner? What kind of condition is your car in? Why are you selling the car? Do you know of any problems with the car? Has it ever been in an accident?"

❀ Check to make sure all the panels are lined up correctly, make sure there are no major dents, make sure the color of the paint matches evenly on every part of the car. If there are any imperfections in these areas it could signal that the car has been in an accident.

❀ Examine the car extensively. Check the tires. Look for leaking fluids. Check under the hood. If you spot a sprayed black film on the underside, this could be indicative of an oil leak or off-kilter oil pressure – two messy hassles you want to avoid! A variety of stickers should be located on the driver's side door. These stickers indicate the car's year, make, model, tire pressure, etc. If these stickers are missing it is a sure sign the paneling has been replaced.

❀ Start the car in front of the buyer. Does it start easily? Do any dashboard lights come on indicating a problem?

❀ Check the car's fluids. (See next section if you are unsure how to do this.) The oil is the lifeblood of the car. If it has not been properly and regularly changed every couple thousand miles, you can be sure that the engine has suffered as a result. Also, check the brake fluid. This is located under the hood in the back right-hand area. Remove the rubber cap so you can check the level of the fluid. You will be able to tell by looking at it if it's okay.

❀ Take the car for a test drive and see how the brakes and steering feel. Listen for any odd noises. Make sure you are comfortable with the look and feel of the vehicle.

❀ Most importantly, have a mechanic look the car over for you. Ask them about any concerns you may have and ask them what they think about purchasing the car. Lastly, make sure the vehicle passes your state's inspections and emissions tests.

HOW TO CHECK YOUR OIL

In order to keep your car in great shape, you should change your oil every 3 months or 3,000 miles. If you aren't sure when you're due, here's how to check. . . .

Step 1: You need to check your oil when the engine has cooled, but is still warm. Checking the oil immediately after driving will give you an inaccurate reading of your oil level because the oil was just in motion. Make sure you are on level ground and the car is turned off. Pop the hood.

Step 2: Next you need to find the dipstick. It is usually located near the engine, which

is near the spark plugs. (If that doesn't ring any bells, then check your owner's manual; it will tell you where to find the dipstick.) Pull the loop up and out. Wipe off the long metal shaft with a rag.

Top 5 Fastest Cars

1. McLaren - 240 mph
2. Lister Storm - 210 mph
3. Lamborghini Diablo GT - 200 mph
4. Ferrari 550 Maranello - 199 mph
5. Renault Espace F1 - 194 mph

According to *The Top Ten of Everything 2001*

Step 3: Reinsert the clean dipstick all the way and when you pull it out, look at the pointy end. There are grooves within the dipstick that indicate if the oil level is correct. Generally there is a three-tiered measurement on the dipstick – low, normal, and full. Your oil level should be within the top and bottom of the lines. If it is your first time checking your oil, you should consult your car manual or ask a gas station attendant for

Quick Tips on How to Spend Less on Gas

1. Use cruise control on the highway.

2. Turn off the engine when you are waiting for more than five minutes.

3. Accelerate slowly from stop signs and lights.

4. Keep your tires inflated to their proper size.

5. Get your car tuned-up every 30,000 miles and change the air filter every 15,000 miles.

6. Four-wheel-drive cars and SUVs tend to have really low gas mileage when compared to front-wheel-drive cars and sedans.

7. Get comfortable in your seat – this will encourage you to press lighter on the gas pedal.

8. Carpool!

help. That way, you can be sure you're doing it correctly.

HOW TO JUMP-START A CAR

So, you left your car lights on the night before and now you're stuck. The battery is as dead as a doornail. Have no fear, here's the easy 5-step method for jump-starting your car. . . .

Step 1: It's really not a bad idea to have a set of jumper cables tucked away in your trunk, especially if you drive an older car. Buy a good set of 100% copper heavy gauge cables that are at least 10 feet long. (They are sold at any car accessory store.) The first thing to do if you don't have cables is to find someone who does. If nobody's in the immediate vicinity, find a pay phone and call a friend. Either way, you'll need some kind person to help you so that he or she can provide the other car.

Step 2: Next, open the hood and take a look

at the battery. (**Note – If there are cracks in the battery casing, do not try to jump it. It could be dangerous. So, leave it be and call a tow truck.) If there is any residue on the battery, clean it off with a rag. But keep in mind that batteries contain sulfuric acid, something you should definitely steer clear of. Be careful!

Step 3: Attaching the cables. Make sure both cars have the same voltage battery and both ignitions are off. Every battery has two terminals, a negative (- black) and a positive (+ red). Attach the positive red cable to the dead battery's positive receptor and then attach the other end of the same cable to the positive terminal on the working car. Next, attach the negative black cable to the working battery and then attach the other end of the same cable to the black negative receptor on the dead battery.

Step 4: As a safety precaution, step back from cars. Next, start the car providing the jump, wait a moment and then try to start the dead car. If it does not start up, wait a little longer and then try it again. If it is in fact battery trouble, your car should start. If it doesn't, the problem is probably not battery related. So have a tow truck number handy.

Step 5: Once you have successfully started the dead battery, disconnect the cables in the exact reverse order you connected them: negative black cable from dead battery, negative black from working battery, positive red

---

Top 5 Selling Cars of All Time

1. Toyota Corolla
2. Volkswagen Beetle
3. Lada Riva
4. Volkswagen Golf
5. Ford Model T

According to *The Top Ten of Everything 2001*
(Information is based on the year each model was produced and the estimated number that was made.)

from working battery, positive red from dead battery. Make sure to leave the car that needed the jump running. Make sure to drive the car for at least 15 miles at highway speed before turning it off again. If battery trouble occurs often, it may be time for a new one. (**Note – If your car battery is older than four years, it needs to be replaced.)

CAR EMERGENCIES

One night at summer camp (while working as counselors), Jenn and I decided to relax and drive to the top of a nearby mountain for stargazing and fresh mountain air. After chatting for hours and catching up on camp gossip, we decided it was time to head back. I turned the ignition to the start position and nothing happened. Trying not to panic, I tried again but to no avail. There we were . . . stuck on the mountain at nightfall, two girls alone, and no cell phone. We got

lucky. After an hour or so, kids from the neighboring camp passed by and we flagged them down for a lift back to camp. We were careless and clueless and had taken no precautions. We don't want you to experience a similar mishap. Whether you break down or run out of gas, there are some key things to remember.

❀ When pulling over, pull to the far edge of the shoulder or a rest stop if possible. If you pull over roadside, be sure that your car is not in a hazardous position for approaching cars.

❀ Turn your hazards on and put up the hood. This will alert drivers that you have a breakdown.

❀ When you pull over roadside, note your location. If you are in a well-lit urban area, then you can easily lock your doors and use your cell phone, or go to a nearby pay-phone. If you are in a remote location it could be dangerous to leave the vehicle. In that case, sit tight with your hazards on.

❀ Be safe! If a stranger approaches to help, stay inside the car with the doors locked. Open the window a crack and ask the person to contact the police for you. Don't leave the car and start walking.

❀ As a precaution, keep an emergency roadside kit in your car. Items to include: a flashlight, blanket, jumper cables, a package of flares, a pen and paper to make a "contact police" sign, a magazine to pass the time and maybe even a snack for your growling tummy.

Sometimes, car problems can be too cumbersome for fix-it-yourself remedies. If that's the case, you need a good mechanic. Of course you don't want to be ripped off and go in for a simple oil change and leave with a brand new engine. Here are some ways to find the best mechanic for your car. . . .

HOW TO FIND A GOOD BODY SHOP

Step 1: The first thing you should do is ask for referrals from friends or coworkers who have the same car as you.

Step 2: Make sure the shop is accredited by the American Automobile Association (AAA).

Step 3: Ask if the mechanics are certified by the National Institute for Automotive Service Excellence (ASE).

Step 4: Check the warranty on all of your repair work and ask for a full explanation of the work that your car needs.

Step 5: Check to see if any complaints have been filed with the Better Business Bureau.

Develop a good relationship with your mechanic. Also, never tell a mechanic what *you* think the problem is. It can be

standard procedure to replace what you have noted as the problem, even though there may be no need.

The "Penny Test" for Tires

When you need to figure out if your tires are too worn down, the Lincoln penny test is one of our favorite tricks. Simply stick a penny into the grooves of your tire with Lincoln's head pointing into the tire. If you can see the top of his head, it's time to buy a new tire!

Gasoline is used as fuel for internal-combustion engines, the engines found in almost every passenger car on the market. Some basics: the higher the octane level, the greater amount of pure gas that's being burned. So the 87, 89, or 93 you see at the gas station represents the octane level of that particular gas line. It can be useful to use a higher octane level on older cars. Newer models, however, run just fine on the lower levels.

DE-ICING YOUR WINDOWS

Jenn called me in November of this year because she was in shock about the severity of her first "bad" Wisconsin winter. Not only did she have cabin fever, she couldn't drive anywhere because the ice on her windshield seemed as though it wouldn't melt until June. We found some effective methods to de-ice your front window. With these freeze-fighting pointers, you'll be driving through the snow in no time!

❀ Leave your windshield wipers in mid-sweep the night before. This makes it easier for them to get the ice off the next day.

❀ Turn the heat level to high and the defroster to low. If the defroster is on too high, it could crack the windshield.

❀ You can make a home de-icing formula of 50% water and 50% vinegar. Spray it onto the windshield and get ready to scrape.

❀ As you scrape the ice away, use downward strokes so you don't scratch the glass. A credit card can work as a scraper if you don't have a real one.

❀ Check your local auto accessory story and ask the clerk to help you find a solution you can apply to your windshield to help de-ice it.

We doubt that women merely want to spend their time learning automobile trivia, but the essentials covered in this chapter could prove to be a huge help if your find yourself in a crunch. So ladies, take heed! Also, always keep your owner's manual in your glove compartment (along with your copy of the *Girl's Guide*) for further information and assistance. On a final note, don't let men tell you that women can't drive. It is a known fact that men get in more accidents every year than women, which is why their insurance premiums are so much higher than ours.

SPORTS

Clumsy to the core, Sam and I have never been quite the athletic type. In high school we tried adopting the "jock mentality" by being cheerleaders, managers of the soccer team (Sam even trained with them!), and by working on our yearbook's sports section. All to no avail. However, due to our inabilities, we have learned to become great spectators and we now appreciate a good Saturday football game or a nail-biting basketball game. So, drawing from our own experiences, here are a few easy-to-understand directions for the sport-illiterate female.

FOOTBALL

When we began writing this book, a guy friend of ours suggested we include a portion for you lovely ladies about Super Bowl-party survival techniques. Typically, Super Bowl Sunday and college football Saturdays consist of guys gathering to drink beer, cheer for their team and focus on the game play by play. Does such a virile crew of football fans like to be distracted by chatting women? Of course not. So, ladies, don't spoil the game for your male buddies. If you're like most females, perhaps you're not clear on the logistics of the sport. If that's the case, have no fear. We've got you covered, play by play. In order to wow your boyfriend or buddy with your newfound appreciation for the pigskin, simply read on.

Tip 1: Football's basic premise is that each team is trying to get the ball into the opponent's end zone as many times as possible, and each time they do, they score. They can get the ball into the "end zone" by passing the ball or running the ball. (Also, field goals result in three points and technically don't involve the ball crossing the goal line in possession of a player.)

Tip 2: Each team has 11 players on the field at any given time, but they are constantly making substitutions because players are designated to play either defense (the other team has the ball) or offense (they have the ball), or on special teams.

Tip 3: When the team has the ball, they have four plays ("downs") to get the ball at least ten yards closer to the other team's end zone. Once a team succeeds at getting the ball at least that far, they get four more chances to get the ball further down the field. Either they do this until they score, or they lose possession of the ball.

VOCABULARY

NFL: The National Football League, NFL, is divided into two conferences: the American Football Conference, the AFC, and the National Football Conference, the NFC. These two conferences are then broken down into three divisions: Eastern, Central, and Western.

Line of Scrimmage: Imaginary line through the ball and parallel to the goal lines. It separates the offense and defense at the beginning of each play.

Special teams: Refers to any part of the game that is not simply offense or defense, be it a kickoff, kick return, punt, field goal or any other play during which a change of possession is expected.

Flag: A yellow handkerchief weighted in the center. When thrown by officials, it means an infraction has occurred; a team is then penalized by the loss of a down, a loss of yardage, or both.

Interception: A passed ball intended for an offensive receiver but caught by the defense, resulting in a change of possession.

The Line: A term used when gambling on football. It deals with the margin by which the winning team is predicted to beat the losing team.

POINT VALUES OF FOOTBALL

Touchdown, 6 points: The ball crosses the plane of the goal line a) while in possession of a player or b) is caught by a player in the end zone.

Extra Point, 1 point: After a touchdown, the team gets the chance to kick the ball through the uprights from the 2½ yard line. (The uprights are the two bars at the back of the 10-yard-deep end zone.)

Field Goal, 3 points: When a team is on their fourth down or only has a few seconds left in the game to score, they try to kick the ball through the uprights instead of attempting a touchdown.

Conversion, 2 points: After a team makes a touchdown, they can try to run the ball into the end zone from the 2½ yard line rather than going for the extra point.

Safety, 2 points: When the defense forces the offense to down the ball in their own end zone or the ball carrier is tackled or steps out of bounds from the end zone.

HOW TO FAKE IT

In order to "talk the talk" of sports, you really don't even need to watch a game. If you spend time reading the sports section or watching a few minutes of ESPN's *SportsCenter*, you'll be amazed at how many tid-bits you can absorb. In football,

learn the names of key players, namely the quarterback, and you'll be able to sound like a pro. And finally, when you really want to get some information on the latest happenings in the sports world, go to a sports bar where patrons are eager

Fun Facts

Person who scored the most single-season touchdowns

In 1995, Dallas Cowboy running back Emmitt Smith scored 25 single-season touchdowns.

~

Superbowl with the highest attendance

Superbowl XIV, January 20th, 1980. The Pittsburgh Steelers vs. the Los Angeles Rams in the Rosebowl in Pasadena, California. The game drew 103,985 people. The Steelers beat the Rams 31-19, becoming the first team to ever win four Superbowls.

to share their knowledge of the game over a few cold ones. Truth be told, this can work for any sport. Throw in a reference or two about *Sports Illustrated*'s most recent cover and you'll sound like a true sports junkie!

When Sam and I used to cheerlead in high school, there was a cheer that went, "First and ten, Raiders, go-fight-win!" Now, we had no clue what "first and ten" meant at the time, but it sounded catchy and it was what our captain taught us, so we did it. We now know that "first and ten" means that the team we were cheering for had gotten a first down and needed to advance down the field ten yards in order to get another first down.

"GO 'BAMA, ROLL TIDE!"

Football Trivia

How many teams are currently in the NFL?

30

~

How big is a football field?

53½ yards wide and 120 yards long

~

Which teams played in the first college bowl game?

Michigan vs. Stanford, January 1, 1902, in the Rose Bowl. Michigan beat Stanford 49-0. Due to the uneven score, the officials of the Tournament of Roses decided to try something else and replaced the game with Roman-style chariot races until football's return in 1916. The Rose Bowl had been built with 57,000 seats and by 1920, the original stands had become too small for the crowds. The stadium now seats 93,000.

Born September 11, 1913, Paul "Bear" Bryant, one of the most legendary college coaches of our time, could not be left out of this book. He is our best friend's godfather, Jenn's stepdad's college coach, and an idol for all of our friends at the University of Alabama. He played end for the Crimson Tide from 1933 to 1935 and then returned as the head coach in 1958. Known for his years of dedication and strict coaching at "Bama," Bear Bryant is one of college football's biggest legends.

The Rose Bowl is home to many other "firsts," including:

The first wirephoto transmission of a Bowl Game (1925)

≈

The first transcontinental radio broadcast of sporting event (1927)

≈

The first National telecast of a college football game (1948)

≈

The Rose Bowl Game has been nicknamed the "Granddaddy of Them All" and has been sold out every year since 1947. The Rose Bowl will host the National Championship Game in 2002.

≈

How many people have won both the Heisman Trophy and the Super Bowl MVP?

Four: Roger Staubach, Jim Plunkett, Marcus Allen, and Desmond Howard

≈

O.J. Simpson is the only player to win the Heisman Trophy and the Pro Bowl MVP. He won the Heisman in 1968 when he played for USC and he won the Pro Bowl MVP in 1973 when he played for the Bills.

❀ He holds the record for the most bowl games as a coach – 24 of them!

❀ His first bowl appearance was in the Great Lakes Bowl in 1947.

❀ He received a scholarship from the University of Alabama without getting a high school degree.

❀ He became the winningest coach for the NCAA Division I in 1981.

❀ He spent 25 seasons at the University of Alabama (1958-1982), winning or sharing 13 of the Southeast Conference Championships. Prior to his 'Bama days, he coached at the University of Maryland (1945), the University of Kentucky (1946-1953) and Texas A&M (1954-1957).

❀ He holds the record for the most bowl game wins, 12 . . . as well as the most bowl game losses, 10. His remaining two bowl appearances both ended in a tie.

BASEBALL

Diamonds may be a girl's best friend, but when it comes to baseball diamonds, American men are right at home. So ladies, it's time to learn to enjoy cold beer, Cracker Jack, the smell of ballpark hot dogs, and the thrill of home runs!

Baseball's essentials are fairly easy to understand, so we're not going into all the details. Here are a few basics to remember when watching a game:

Baseball is played on a field consisting of a grassy outfield and a dirt-covered infield, where most of the action takes place. The infield is shaped like a diamond, marked by 4 bases that indicate the route for an offen-

Fun Facts

World's all-time leading home-run hitter
Hank Aaron of the Atlanta Braves. He hit 755 homeruns during his twenty-four year career (1952-1976).

~

Most career strikeouts
Nolan Ryan, who played for the New York Mets, the California Angels, the Houston Astros, and the Texas Rangers. He had 5,714 strikeouts in his 27-year career.

~

World's longest baseball game
Brooklyn Dodgers vs. the Boston Braves, May 1, 1920. The game lasted 26 innings, with a constant 1-1 tie. Officials finally ended the game because it became too dark. Both pitchers played the entire game.

sive player. A pitcher stands in the middle of the infield diamond and pitches to the batter, who stands at home plate. A player is considered "safe" once he reaches a base without getting out. A run is scored once a player makes it all the way around the diamond back to home plate. Each game is nine innings long with each inning consisting of

both teams getting as many players up to bat as possible before their team gets 3 outs.

WAYS A PLAYER CAN BE CALLED "OUT"

1) The batter hits a fair or foul ball that is caught before it hits the ground.

2) A batter receives 3 strikes.

3) The batter is tagged with the ball.

4) An opposing player touches the base while holding the ball before the batter reaches the base.

5) Force play – When every base previous to the base being tagged has a runner on it during the at-bat.

PITCHING POSSIBILITIES

The pitcher can try a number of different pitches in his attempt to strike out the bat-

Man of the Hour

BABE RUTH

~

Babe Ruth, one of the most famous baseball players in history ended his career with a .690 batting average. He holds the lifetime records for home run percentages and walks, and was one of the first five players to be inducted into the Baseball Hall of Fame.

ter. Whether it's a curve ball or a fast ball, it's necessary for the pitcher to throw the ball within a certain zone, the strike zone (typically just wider than home plate and from the "letters" across the batter's chest down to his knees). If the pitch is outside of the strike zone, the umpire will consider it a "ball."

VOCABULARY

MLB: Major League Baseball (MLB) is divided into two leagues, the American

League (AL), and the National League (NL). In each league, the teams are divided into 3 divisions: West, Central, and East.

Ball: A pitched ball that misses the strike zone.

Count: The number of balls and strikes on a batter. If a pitcher has more strikes than balls on a batter, he is "ahead of the count." If he has more balls than strikes on a batter, he is "behind in the count."

Full Count: When the pitcher has thrown 2 strikes and 3 balls to the player at bat. The pitch count is full, meaning another ball results in a walk and another strike results in an out.

Double Play: Two outs executed by fielders in one play.

Grand Slam: A home run that is hit when the bases are loaded, resulting in four runs.

Batting average: The number of hits a batter gets divided by the number of times he comes up to bat.

Baseball Trivia

How many consecutive division titles have the Atlanta Braves won? (as of 2000)

7

~

On July 17, 1941, Joe DiMaggio's 56-game hit streak came to an end against what team?

Cleveland Indians

~

What team boasts the only perfect game pitched in World Series history?
New York Yankees pitcher Don Larson pitched a perfect game in 1956 against the Brooklyn Dodgers.

~

Who hit the longest home run in history?
Mickey Mantle – 643 feet

ABBREVIATIONS TO KNOW

BASKETBALL

RBI: Runs Batted In

HR: Home runs

ERA: Earned Runs Average – An average of how many runs are scored against a pitcher in nine innings.

Fun Facts

Teams with the most World Series wins (as of 2000)

1. New York Yankees – 26 wins

2. St. Louis Cardinals and Philadelphia Kansas City/Oakland Athletics – 9 wins

3. Brooklyn/LA Dodgers – 6 wins

~

In 1860, the Cincinnati Red Stockings became the first baseball team to receive a regular salary. Their salaries ranged from $800 to $1400 a season. Today's players are making an average of $3 million a year.

Yet another of our failed athletic attempts was when Sam and I played basketball for our youth group. Between the two of us, we made three baskets the entire season and one of those was in the other team's basket. (We won't say which one of us did that!) Pathetic, we know. Although we didn't learn how to become professional basketball players, we did manage to learn a few things about the sport.

Currently, the women's NBA (WNBA) is gaining popularity, prompting more women to pay attention to the sport. Men's basketball, however, remains faster, tougher, and more popular than women's. The game of basketball is based on which team scores the highest number of baskets. Thus, the game's main competition centers around possession of the ball. Each team has five players on the court at a time and different players have different positions:

Point Guard: The player who brings the ball down the court and who directs the offense.

Shooting Guard: A position filled by players skilled in ball handling and dribbling who cover the perimeter of the offensive and defensive zones.

Center: Most often one of the tallest players on the court, who defends and plays "the paint," the area right in front of the basket.

Forwards: (2 – Strong/Power Forward and Small Forward) The two players who cover the corner areas on the sides of the basket.

There are also two kinds of defense that are important to know:

Man-to-Man: Each defender guards an opposing player wherever he goes on the court.

Zone: Each defender defends a specific area of the court and guards any and all opposing players that enter that area.

VOCABULARY

NBA: The National Basketball Association, NBA, is divided into two conferences, the Western Conference and the Eastern Conference. Each conference is divided into two divisions: the Pacific Division and the Midwest Division in the West, and the Central Division and the Atlantic Division in the East.

Dribble: To bounce the ball in a series of successive taps. A player cannot walk with the ball unless he or she is dribbling it. Once the ball comes to rest in one or both hands, the player must stop moving.

Rebound: To gain possession of a ball which hits the basket but doesn't go in.

Free throw: An unhindered shot from behind the free-throw line that is awarded when a player is fouled.

Key: Short for keyhole, it consists of the area at each end of the court marked by the free-throw line and the restraining circle around it. A player can spend no more than 3 seconds in the paint without being penalized.

5 LEGENDARY BASKETBALL PLAYERS TO KNOW AND WHY

(Based on an informal poll of our guy friends.)

1.Bill Russell
NBA Team: Boston Celtics (1956-1969)
Position: Center
Why you should know him: Five-time NBA MVP and twelve-time All-Star. He took the Celtics to the championships 11 of his 13 years with the team. He was voted Greatest Player in the History of the NBA by the Professional Basketball Writers Association of America.

2.Wilt Chamberlain ("The Big Dipper")
NBA Team: Philadelphia Warriors, who later became the Philadelphia 76ers (1959-1973)
Position: Guard
Why you should know him: He was the only NBA player to score 4,000 points in one season. He once scored 100 points in one game and got 55 rebounds in another. He has the second highest point total of any player in the U.S. Standing at 7'1" and weighing in at over 300 pounds, he could dominate in the paint like no other.

3. Kareem Abdul-Jabbar
NBA Team: Milwaukee Bucks (1969-1975) and LA Lakers (1975-1989)
Position: Center
Why you should know him: When Kareem left the game in 1989 at 42 years old, no other NBA player had ever scored more points, blocked more shots, won more MVP awards, played in more All-Star Games, or performed at an older age. He

holds the record for the most career field goals (any shot other than a free throw or a three-pointer). He was a member of 6 NBA championship teams. Famous for his "sky hook" shot, he left the game with 38,387 points.

Basketball Trivia

What kind of baskets were originally used in basketball?
Peach baskets

Who was the first player to jump directly from high school ball to the pros?
Moses Malone. He was 19 when he signed as the center for the Utah Jazz.

What is the name and age of the youngest player to score 50 points in a NBA game?
Rick Barry. In 1965, he was 21 years old while playing for the San Francisco Warriors. It was his first year of professional ball after playing at the University of Miami.

4. Earvin "Magic" Johnson

NBA Team: LA Lakers (1979-1992)
Position: Point Guard
Why you should know him: Magic is 6'9", making him the tallest point guard in history. With his behind-the-back and no-look passes, as well as his ability to put away half-court shots, he was a dynamic player to watch. He was a member of 5 championship teams, the recipient of 3 MVP awards, and a member of the original 1992 gold medal-winning "Dream Team." He had to retire from the NBA due to testing positive for the HIV virus in 1992, but returned for one more season in 1995.

5. Michael Jordan

NBA Team: Chicago Bulls (1984-1994)
Position: Guard
Why you should know him: He was selected in 1996 as one of the top 50 NBA players of all time. He received the NBA's MVP award 5 times, and he was on the Olympic basketball

gold-medal team in 1984 and 1992. One of the sport's all-time greatest players, he averaged 31.5 points per game. ESPN named him "The Athlete of the Century." Ironically, he was cut from his high school's basketball team as a sophomore. To remind him of his college days, he always wore his University of North Carolina shorts under his Bulls uniform for good luck.

GOLF

The game of golf is probably the easiest to understand, but many say the hardest to master. It is another sport that is drawing more women players these days, yet there still remain countless golf clubs throughout the United States where women are not allowed to play or are only allowed tee times after men. However, since they say that golf is all about patience, concentration, and practice, we know that this is the perfect sport for women!

The men in Sam's family are completely "golf obsessed." Her brother, father, and uncle talk about it incessantly, play every free minute they have, and when they're tired, they simply watch it on TV. Golf is played with a small, hard ball and a set of clubs, the object being to hit the ball a long distance over a grassy course into a series of 18 holes with the fewest possible strokes. Some courses have 9 holes, but most regulation courses have 18. Golf is usually played in twosomes or foursomes and each player hits his or her own ball.

VOCABULARY

PGA: Professional Golf Association

Par: A standard number of strokes that an expert playing errorless golf would be expected to make. In golf's origins in

Scotland, "par" was designated only to an entire round of golf, not to individual holes. Only when golf's popularity reached America was an individual hole given its own number for par.

Birdie: One stroke under par

Bogey: One stroke over par

Eagle: Two strokes under par

Handicap: An advantage given to a weak opponent or a disadvantage given to a strong opponent to allow competitors of different abilities to compete on even ground.

Majors: The 4 major golf tournaments. They are the British Open, the U.S. Open, the Masters, and the PGA Championship. Of these 4 majors, the Masters is the only one played on the same course every year, Augusta National. The other 3 tournaments occur in different locations each year.

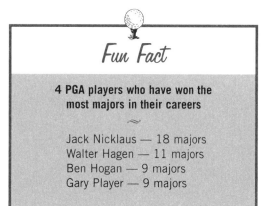

Fun Fact

4 PGA players who have won the most majors in their careers

Jack Nicklaus — 18 majors
Walter Hagen — 11 majors
Ben Hogan — 9 majors
Gary Player — 9 majors

AREAS AROUND THE GOLF COURSE

Tee: The area where a ball is driven from at the beginning of each hole. Courses generally have different starting points for players of different levels.

Fairway: Grassy playing area between the tee and the green (typically mowed to ⅓ of an inch) that ranges from 250 to 350 yards.

Putting Green: The area of finely manicured grass where the hole (4½ inches in diameter) is located and marked by a flagstick.

Rough: The "first cut" of grass off the fair-way and green.

Bunker/Sand-trap: A hazard on the course, usually located near the green. Consists of a large man-made indentation filled with loose sand.

Water Hazard: Any sea, lake, pond, river, ditch, surface draining ditch, or anything of a similar nature (whether or not containing water). Marked by yellow or red (lateral water hazard) stakes.

THE SCOOP ON TIGER WOODS

Tiger was born on September 30, 1975. He made his first television appearance – golf clubs in tow – at the mere age of 3 on the *Mike Douglas Show*. After playing golf for Stanford University, Woods went pro in September 1996 and won the fifth event he ever entered. In his first full year on tour, he won 6 out of 25 events. Tiger set a

record at the 1997 Masters for shooting 18 under par and then set a U.S. Open record in 2000 when he won by 15 strokes at Pebble Beach. Not only was he the youngest player to win at Augusta, he was the first African-American to take home the Masters trophy. He caused television ratings to increase more than 50% for the final rounds of the four 1997 majors. Woods' recent dominance in the world of golf has prompted PGA publicity and popularity to skyrocket.

Fun Fact

Top 5 money-winning golfers of all time (as of 11/13/00)

Tiger Woods — $20,503,450
Davis Love, III — $14,828,227
Phil Mickelson — $13,434,115
Nick Price — $13,190,669
Greg Norman — $13,087,832

TYPES OF CLUBS

There are many different types of clubs a golfer can use on the course. Basically, you choose a club based on the yardage that you need to cover to get closer to the hole.

The fundamental difference between clubs comes down to one thing: degree of loft. Each wood and iron has a different degree, which is designed to take a golfer's swing and project it a certain distance. The driver (a wood) is between 8 and 11 degrees, making it the longest club in the bag. Wedges are between 54 and 70 degrees and are used for lofty shorter shots. The loft of these wedges is also important in enabling a golfer to "drop" the ball onto the green. As far as structure, irons are thinner than woods and their club heads are referred to as blades.

The USGA Rules mandate that a player may have no more than 14 clubs in his or her bag. While each player may select differently in accordance with his personal preference, the typical selection is as follows: 2 to 9 irons, a driver, 3 wood, 5 wood, wedge, sand wedge, and last but not least, a putter.

Fun Fact

Only 5 players have won all four Grand Slam titles

~

Tiger Woods
Jack Nicklaus
Ben Hogan
Gary Player
Gene Sarazen

* Only one player has won all four Majors in a single year: In 1930, amateur Bobby Jones won the U.S. Amateur, the British Amateur, the U.S. Open, and the British Open – the 4 major tourneys at that time. He later went on to found the Masters.

Golf Trivia

When and at which tournament did Tiger Woods turn pro?
August 27, 1996, at the Greater Milwaukee Open. With a final score of 277, 7 under par, he tied for 60th place.

~

When did the Ryder Cup competition begin?
1927

~

Name 2 records held by Byron Nelson.
Most consecutive tournaments won and most wins in a calendar year.
He had 11 consecutive wins in 1945. That same year,
he won 18 out of the 30 tournaments in which he competed,
including the PGA Championship.

~

Who is the youngest golfer to win a major?
A Scottish lad named "Young" Tom Morris was 17 years old when
he won the first of 4 consecutive opens in 1868 in Scotland.

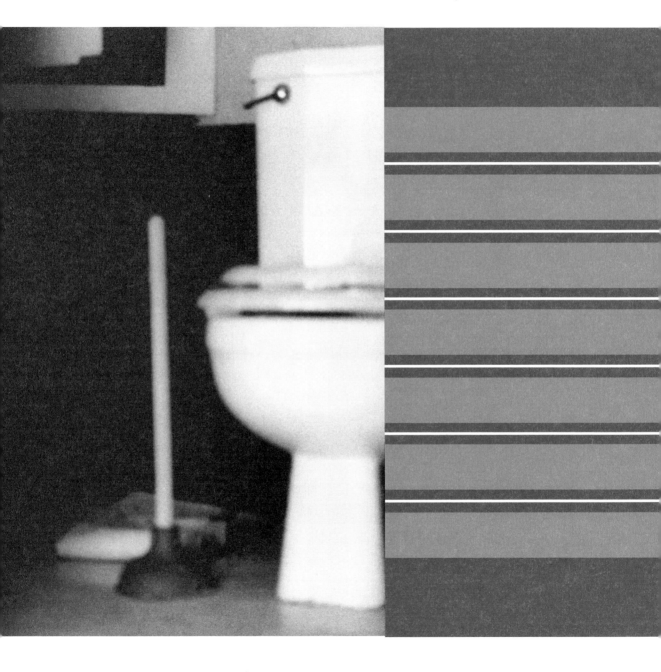

AROUND THE HOUSE

One summer, Jenn and I enrolled at UC–Berkeley to study for the semester. We found a cheap, ramshackle place to rent. Talk about a fixer-upper! Getting the right tools definitely would've helped us as we got settled. We soon realized that Jenn's black boots with the four-inch wedge heel were not doing the trick as a makeshift hammer around the house. Girls, it is imperative to have the correct tools in order to deal with your household projects . . . no matter how basic they may seem.

Since leaving home for college almost four years ago, the two of us have lived in a total of eleven different residences.

Each of our homes has had its fair share of problems that needed some basic form of repair. Actually, prior to this book, household maintenance was not our forte. In fact, it was during the course of one dreadful move-in that the concept for the book took shape. Our research has proved eye-opening and we now are quite the valuable assets to our other house-mates. Don't be misled – we are far from being handywomen. We are, however, well-versed in basic maintenance. This chapter is loaded with information that will humble your carpenter, intrigue your plumber, shock your electrician, and most importantly impress your male friends. So, ladies, when faced with a household disaster, don't automatically reach for your handyman's phone number. Instead, take a deep breath, skim through these pages and follow our simple "fix-it-yourself" tips.

THE BASIC TOOLBOX

Nails and Screws: They come in a variety of types and sizes. Screws have greater holding power than nails and are designed with different grooves on the ends to accept differing types of screwdrivers.

Screwdriver: A hand tool used to insert screws into various objects. A Philips screwdriver is a screwdriver with a pointed tip that has a cross on the end of it. A flat-head screwdriver has a tip that is flat and comes to a solid line at the end.

Wrench: A wrench is used to tighten nuts and bolts. An adjustable wrench allows you to work with a number of different-sized nuts and bolts. A Monkey wrench is one where the jaws are positioned at a right angle from the handle. It gets its name from its inventor, Charles Moncky.

Carpenter's level: A tool that is used to

determine if a surface is level. (It's that ruler that has the bubbles in it.)

Carpenter's Hammer: A hammer made for driving in and pulling out nails.

Toilet Plunger: A shaft (often wooden) with a molded rubber cup affixed to the end, used to dislodge blockages in plumbing lines.

~

Renovating a "fixer upper" can be fun and rewarding work, but there are a few things you need to remember. Most importantly, be safe, use common sense, and don't be afraid to get down and dirty. Don't try to tackle a project if you have no idea where to begin. And be realistic – some tasks may be too complicated for an amateur. Remember that the product directions, though notoriously intimidating, can be your greatest ally. Finally, visit your local hardware store, bat your sweet eyelashes at the salespeople and pick their brains. They are often a great resource and can answer most of your questions. Make friends with those guys! They work long, hard days. Furthermore, many hardware stores offer free "how-to" sessions in the evenings. Drop in on one . . . it's a great way to brush up on your carpentry skills (or lack thereof) and maybe even meet some cute guys.

~

Moving into a new house or apartment can be the most difficult part of the entire house-maintenance procedure. To avoid a moving-day headache, follow the checklist below.

❀ Obtain a credit report to give to tentative new landlords.

❀ Figure out which of your possessions you are keeping, throwing away, or storing. A garage sale is a great idea for those old belongings you no longer need.

❀ Give at least a four-week notice to your current landlord before moving.

❀ Cancel your monthly bills and notify the post office about your change of address several weeks before you move.

❀ Label all your boxes so your moving and unpacking process is easier.

❀ Back up all your computer files onto a disk.

❀ Defrost and clean out your refrigerator.

HOW TO HANG A PICTURE

Whether it's a photo of your best buds from high school, a print of your favorite Renoir, or a life-size poster of Brad Pitt, each picture deserves to be hung properly. It can make or break any room in your home. For lightweight objects you can simply use a standard picture hanger. If you are going to hang a heavy mirror or perhaps attach a shelf, you will need to affix your bolt into a stud – a support inside the wall on which the dry wall is hung. Studs are often made of either metal or wood, depending on the age of the home, and they are usually 16 to 20 inches apart. Tap on the wall with two knuckles. When tapping, you should hear a succession of hollow sounds, followed by a "non-hollow" sound. The tap that yields a non-hollow sound indicates the home of the stud. If this "tap-and-seek" method proves too difficult, you can purchase a stud-finder from your local hardware shop. While we wish this tool was a way to locate hot guys, it really is a battery operated device that uses magnets to seek the nails found within the stud.

Step 1 The first thing you need to do when hanging a picture is to survey the wall and find that perfect spot.

Step 2 Next, you want to check out the back of the picture. Make sure the wire is securely anchored to the frame, and that it is strong enough to support the weight of the frame.

Step 3 O.K., the next thing you want to do is grab a pencil and tuck it behind your ear. Now hold the picture with one hand on the wire and the other hand holding the bottom of the frame. Hook your finger under the wire in the center so that the picture hangs straight. By doing this you will leave an indentation on the wire and that is where the hook will hold the picture. Hold the picture up to the wall and make sure it is centered and straight. This is when a girl-friend will come in handy to tell you how it looks from a distance.

Step 4 Now hammer in your nail at about a 45-degree angle so the hook will hang flatly against the wall.

Step 5 Carefully pick up the frame and make sure the wire hangs outward and loops upward. Hold the picture up to the wall well above the hook and then slide it down slow-ly so that the hook catches the wire. Now you can adjust the picture slightly or use a

level to check its straightness.

PAINTING A ROOM

There are times in a girl's life when change is needed. You know what I mean – it's that impetuous moment of whimsy when we color our hair, cut our own bangs, or dou-ble pierce our ears. Sudden change prompted by spontaneous action and little thought. I walked around with pink hair for a week after one of these change-needed episodes. If you're looking for a project that can be a blast, and is sure to give you the change you need, why not paint a room? When we moved into our house senior year, my girlfriend decided her basement room needed a facelift. As so many of our proj-ects go, it was a disaster! The lavender paint eventually made it to the walls, but it also made its way to the carpet, her bed-ding, and all over her curtains. So women, pay attention! Here it is – the foolproof way to get this project done right.

Step 1 Take a trip to the hardware store to seek supplies and advice. Buy the most expensive paint your budget will allow; most often it wears best and makes your work easier. After choosing your color, ask the hardware store to mix the paint for you. Come checkout time, be sure your cart includes an ample amount of primer, paint, and top coat as well as a roller brush for the walls and ceiling and a two-inch brush for your windows and trim.

Step 2 Prepare your pad for the renovation. Move all of your furniture to the center of the room and cover it well with a tarp. Also, cover with masking tape or old bed sheets anything you don't want painted (doorknobs, window trimming, woodwork, carpeting, etc.). Be sure to wash your walls carefully before painting in order to get rid of dirt and grime. Pay special attention to greasy or oily surfaces. Put about a tablespoon of household cleanser in a bucket of hot water, and grab a sponge.

Step 3 When painting, you want to start at the ceiling and work your way down to the floor. This will prevent splattering. The best way to paint the ceiling is by using a roller brush with an extension. After you're done with the ceiling, get started on the walls. It is easiest to paint the corners first using a brush and then paint the rest of the wall with a roller brush using a "W" motion, filling in each "W" as you go. Work with small sections and take your time.

Step 4 Last but not least, it's time to paint the trimmings – the windows, the electrical outlet plates, the doorframes and baseboards. Our advice here is to be patient and precise. A sloppy trim can spoil all your hard work.

SOME MISCELLANEOUS TID-BITS

❀ Keep a rag handy while painting. Dampen the rag with water or thinner depending on what type of paint you're using. If an accident happens, you're prepared.

❀ Try not to sleep in the room if it has just been painted; the fumes can be toxic.

❀ When painting windows, don't make the silly mistake of painting the window while it's closed.

❀ Take your time – painting is a project that can't be rushed. In fact, it may require multiple coats of paint.

❀ There are also cool textures you can do to get a fresh look. Sponge painting can create a fabulous effect in any room. If you are interested, check for some reading material at art and hardware stores.

HOW TO CATCH A MOUSE

If you spot a mouse in your house, it probably means that his friends are somewhere nearby. You need to develop a fast and effective plan to catch the critter. (Your plan need not be as elaborate as our first "plan" below was). After I moved into my current home in College Park, Maryland, my darling friend and roommate Sue saw a little mouse scurry across her bedroom floor while she was studying. Shocked and frightened, she jumped on her bed screaming bloody murder. We unified and mobilized – we were going to be tough and catch the little bugger. The six of us girls blitzed the room wearing goggles, goulashes, and gloves, armed with umbrellas, a trashcan, and spatulas (Don't ask what the spatulas were for – at the time it made sense). We found the mouse and cornered it behind a desk while one girl banged on the trash can and the others held the line, ready to attack. All to no avail. As soon as the mouse appeared we lost our cool and panicked, dashing for the door. We tried again and again and the same thing happened. We would muster up our confidence, infiltrate the enemy territory, and then frantically disperse. As you might imagine, our tactics didn't get us far. After weeks we found that the best method for solving our rodent problem was a simple mousetrap. First and foremost, don't freak out! As gross as this ordeal can be, these little mice cannot hurt you. You are a strong, independent woman, so as much as you want to reach for the phone and call someone, you can tackle this one on your own.

Step 1 Once you've spotted an unwanted furry friend, you need to buy some traps . . . ASAP! The old metal ones shown in cartoons can be a real mess – they don't always kill the animal in one clean sweep. Glue traps can be a nuisance as well. As their name implies, they make the animal stick to the trap, which then forces it to starve to death. Your best bet is a covered trap. The number of traps you will need depends on the size of your problem.

Step 2 Now that you have the traps, you need to strategically place them around your home out of the way of household traffic. Mice prefer to reside in dark spaces, so we suggest placing the traps behind furniture, under sinks, and/or in corners. These irritating critters usually get in through small holes around the plumbing fixtures and through any gaps between the floor and baseboard. If you can locate those entry spots, try covering them with a durable putty-like material or with planks that can be nailed into the wall.

Step 3 Next, you need to bait the trap. Contrary to popular belief, cheese actually doesn't work best as a lure. Peanut butter and chocolate are the way to go. You don't need too much, just a little portion or piece. Try not to touch too much of the lure – you want the mice to smell the bait, not you.

Step 4 Check your traps every morning. If

HOW TO OPEN A JAR

you don't see results in three days, relocate and rebait the traps. You might even try rearranging your furniture. Perhaps the changed layout will direct your furry friend to a nearby trap.

Step 5 If you have set the trap and you find it full, dispose of it. Congratulations! You have not only solved your rodent problem, you have broken the age-old stereotype of your gender's irrational fear of mice.

Disclaimer: This method will not work on unwanted boys. It's best to stop feeding them.

Mouse problems must be dealt with immediately. If they are put on the back burner, a minor situation could explode into a rat-infested nightmare. And ladies, as you well know, creepy critter scenarios can be avoided altogether by keeping your home nice and clean!

When you are famished and that dill pickle looks delicious, it can be quite annoying when the jar lid is impossible to open. Have you ever encountered a gridlock jar that only Arnold Schwarzenegger could muscle open? If so, rest assured – we've all been there. After hundreds of grunts, tries, twists and turns, the lid still won't budge, and your arms feel like cooked spaghetti. Here are some tips that will make that top pop in a zip.

Step 1 Wash your hands and the jar to remove all unwanted residue and dirt. Rinsing the jar with warm water works best.

Step 2 Drape a towel over the lid of the jar and try the twist again. The thinner the towel, the better the results. Or instead of a towel, you can use a rubber gripper, which can be found at any grocery or hardware store.

Step 3 To maximize your strength, hold the jar at chest level and face the back of your hand away from you. Wrap the fingers of your strongest hand around the sides of the jar. Wrap your other hand on the sides of the lid and twist in opposite directions while exhaling slowly.

Or . . . if that didn't work, bang the back of a knife against the lid all the way around the rim, until the lid loosens or you hear a faint pop. You can also bang the top of the container on the ground, counter, or any other hard surface and it should loosen.

HOW TO FIX A STOPPED-UP TOILET

Cotton balls, Q-tips, feminine products, chewing gum, eyeliner shavings . . . many things can cause blockage in your commode. This can be one of the most unappealing jobs for the handywoman. With the proper technique, however, the solution can be quite simple.

Step 1 Turn off the water valve near the base of the toilet. (It's the only thing that looks like it can be turned. Clockwise twisting will turn off the water.)

Step 2 Grab your plunger. The toilet bowl should be half filled with water. Make a tight seal with the plunger over the hole of the outflow. Push down on the plunger and then bring it back to its original position. This plunging forces the water in the pipe forward. Repeat this plunging action 9 to 12 times. If the toilet flushes, then the problem is fixed. If not, repeat this action a couple of times.

Step 3 (for the advanced handywoman) If you feel confident with your fix-it self, then you should get a plumber's snake. A plumber's snake is used to pull clogged objects out of the outflow. Insert the snake into the outflow until it catches on the clogged article. Give a good pull and remove the blocked object. If the object is being stubborn, pull back and forth to try and loosen the object. Once loosened, give another big pull to remove it.

Step 4 If none of the above works then it's time to call the plumber. Some jobs are just too much!

HOW TO FIX A RUNNING TOILET

Jenn and I were at a friend's party one Saturday night, and she came across some essential gossip she had to share with me. She invited me into her office, the bathroom, to discuss the latest news. Sure enough, karma got us back. Dressed in my highest of high heels, I flushed the toilet, and the water level began to rise . . . and rise . . . and rise. Within seconds the toilet was completely overflowing! It was soooooo embarrassing. Perhaps you've suffered through a similarly mortifying experience.

If so, I feel your pain. If not, it's never too soon to be prepared.

Step 1 Take the lid off the toilet and examine the parts.

Step 2 Oftentimes the problem is simple: The large black cap, the stopper, is not properly covering the hole. Simply re-adjust it so that it does cover the entire hole. Or perhaps the stopper is old and deteriorated. As a result, it allows water to seep out of the flush valves seat. If so, it needs replacing.

Step 3 The stopper is held in place by a chain or a thin bar. In order to readjust the stopper's position, simply jiggle the chain or bar until the stopper is correct.

Step 4 For a more permanent solution to the problem, check to see that the bar connected to the stopper is not bent or that the chain is not broken. A quick solution to a broken chain is to make one out of paper clips that will easily hook into the spot where the chain was attached.

Step 5 If these methods are not working, and your toilet is still running, it is probably time to purchase a new stopper. You can grab one at the local hardware store for only a few bucks. Follow the instructions it comes with. It's surprisingly not that difficult.

BLOWING FUSES

As every girl knows, true beauty is found on the inside. Yet, let's be honest ladies, we like to look good on the surface as well. And for that there are countless electrical appliances essential to the beautification process. For us it includes an 1800-watt hairdryer, a blue sapphire hair straightener, a curling iron, an electric toothbrush, a well-lit makeup mirror, and other girly gadgets. So you can see why we have experienced a few power shortages along the way.

While in school at the University of Maryland, my roommates and I experienced power shortages on a regular basis. Without fail, while getting ready for a girls' night out, we always managed to blow a fuse. After weeks of replacing fuses, we insisted that our landlord install a breaker box. Though the box was somewhat helpful, we still had to implement a system for getting ready. Once it came time to blow-dry our locks, the living room lights had to be turned off, the microwave and stereos had to stay off, and a strict no TV policy went into effect. Ultimately, problem solving and ingenuity taught us how to deal with this ongoing problem. But there are many reasons why at some time or another your power might overload. Don't panic! Grab a flashlight. If a portion of your home goes dark, chances are you have simply blown a fuse. Here's how to check. . . .

Step 1 Look around the house for smoke, black smudges, bad plugs, or frayed cords.

If you spot one of these problems, disconnect the bad appliance and repair or replace it. A circuit may also overheat if there are too many appliances running at the same time. An overloaded circuit can be avoided by moving appliances to alternate outlets.

Step 2 Check your circuit breakers or fuse box. If you have circuit breakers, find the switch that is in the off position and return it to on. If you have a fuse box, look in the glass of the fuse to see if the metal is broken or burnt out. If it is, the fuse is blown and needs to be replaced.

Step 3 If you reset the circuit or replace the fuse and it immediately blows again, you may have a wiring short circuit and you will need to call an electrician.

LIVE LIKE BILL GATES, SORT OF . . . AND MAKE TECHNOLOGY WORK FOR YOU

How many times have you been awakened by that blaring alarm clock and not wanted to get out of bed? Wouldn't it be easier if you knew there was hot coffee brewing downstairs? And wouldn't it be great if you could turn your lights on and off by remote control? With this quick-fix technique on how to make anything in your house remote controlled, the lazy can become even lazier. . . .

The source that allows all remote control activity to occur within your house is called X10, or power line carrier signals. There are many types of controls for X10, some with only one button, others that can control many different household appliances. All you need to do to make any appliance remote controlled is to buy a module for the appliance and a controller, which basically looks like a garage door opener. To install the equipment, merely plug the appliance into the module, then plug the module into the wall. With a simple plug extension, the palm of your hand can control your entire house!

With these quick and easy household tips, your home will be picture perfect in days! And more importantly, think of the big bucks you've saved.

Quick Tips

To screw or unscrew basically anything remember ...
"righty-tighty, lefty-loosey."

≈

If you have difficulty getting a plunger to stay over a drain,
wipe it with petroleum jelly to secure a tight seal.

≈

Do your household doors let out an irritating squeak?
If so, say adios to that squeakiness with a can of WD-40.
Simply squirt your door hinges and your problem is solved.

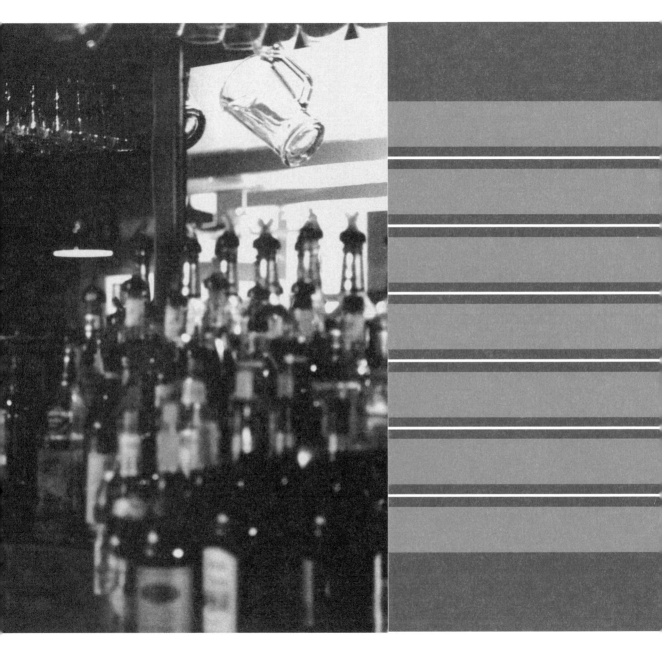

THE BAR

To all the ladies out there who love their screwdrivers and vodka tonics, it's time to learn about what's on tap in the world of the male bar-goer. Mainly, it can be summed up in four letters: B-E-E-R. Though often thought of as a man's drink, beer is becoming more and more popular with the ladies these days. If you want to hang at the bar in typical male fashion, there are a few things you will need to know. We're going to introduce you to the basics of beer, wine, shots, and hard liquor. So get cozy on your barstool and start reading. The next time you find yourself chillin' at the bar, here are some helpful hints.

DRINKING DO'S AND DON'TS

Listen up, dames: Before we delve into the complex subculture of the male bar patron, we have a public service announcement. Preaching we are not – these are the facts and they're not to be taken lightly.

❋ A standard drink is defined as 12 ounces of beer, 5 ounces of wine, or 1.5 ounces of 80 proof distilled spirits, all of which contain the same amount of alcohol.

❋ The legal drinking age in the United States is 21. There are serious repercussions to underage drinking. So be patient and wait for your big birthday before popping open a frosty brew.

❋ Never drink and drive! According to www.madd.org and the National Highway Traffic and Safety Administration (1999), alcohol involvement remains the leading factor in motor-vehicle deaths. Traffic crashes are the greatest single cause of death for every age from 6 to 33 and nearly half of those fatalities happen in alcohol-related crashes. In 1999, 3,609 women were killed in drunk-driving accidents. Men are four times more likely than women to drive after drinking. So, ladies, be careful and always ride with a designated driver.

❋ Women absorb and metabolize alcohol very differently than men. We achieve a higher blood alcohol concentration than men when drinking the same amount of alcohol. We are also more susceptible to alcohol-related organ damage, including damage to the liver and heart. So while this chapter can help you to better understand the world of "manly" drinking, remember at the end of the day you are different and that's what makes you special.

❋ Drink responsibly! Excessive amounts of alcohol can cloud your judgment and make you act irrationally. There are also substantial negative health effects caused by drinking carelessly. Drinking can alter control of your sensory facilities, cause sickness, and even result in memory loss. We could all tell embarrassing stories to illustrate that fact, so be smart and be careful.

These facts aren't intended to scare you, but rather to make you aware. If you heed this advice, then you are ready to be an educated and responsible bar babe, and you will turn heads with your extensive knowledge. Read on.

BEER

Fun Fact

Main Ingredients of Beer

Beer is composed of hops, yeast, barley, and water. Different variations of these ingredients create different types of beer.

VOCABULARY

Ale: Ale is a bitter and stronger-flavored beer, generally dark in color and intense in taste. It is made from top-fermenting yeast. This alcoholic beverage is brewed by the rapid fermentation and infusion of malt and hops. Popular ales include Sierra Nevada Pale Ale or Bass Ale.

Barley: Barley is a basic cereal grain containing enzymes that convert the grain's starch into sugar. To be used in beer, barley must be malted.

Hops: Hops is a flowering vine. Its flowers and essential oils are used as preservatives to add flavor and aroma and to balance out the sweetness of the malt.

Lager: Often light in color and flavor, lagers tend to be highly carbonated and fairly dry. Lagers are brewed by slow bottom fermentation and then matured under refrigeration. Some examples are Budweiser, Red Dog, Rolling Rock, or Samuel Adams.

Malting: Malting allows the grain to germinate (sprout roots). The seed at this time becomes rich in starch. The grain is then heated to a temperature that stops the growth process, but allows the enzyme to remain active. The starch is then converted into sugar. This sugar metabolizes the yeast into carbon dioxide and ethyl alcohol . . . ultimately creating beer.

Stout: An extra dark, top-fermenting brew made of highly roasted malts. There are many different types of stouts. For taste tests, try the Irish classic Guinness. And for sweeter-tasting stout, try Mackeson.

Porter: A well-known London brew that has seen renewed popularity in recent years. It is a lighter-bodied beer resembling a stout. Microbreweries often carry good, original porters. To sample one, visit your local microbrewery.

Pilsner: This type of beer got its name from the town of Pilsen, Bohemia, a Czech province. It is a dry, bottom-fermenting, golden-colored beer. A Pilsner, such as a Bud Light or Miller Lite, generally has a hoppy flavor and a dry finish.

Yeast: Yeast is a unicellular fungi that converts sugar into alcohol. Ale yeast ferments at the "top" of the fermentation vessel at a higher temperature (60 to 75 degrees Fahrenheit) than lager yeast. Lager yeast ferments at a slow pace on the bottom of the fermentation vessel at 34 degrees Fahrenheit.

BEER'S HISTORY

Beer has been around for a very long time. Some experts say that beer may have even been discovered before bread! In fact, historians found evidence that the ancient Sumerian and Mesopotamian peoples consumed beer as far back as 10,000 B.C. Written in Sumerian cuneiform, the first historical records detailing the art of beer-making date back some 4,000 years. The Incas, Mayans, and Aztecs were also brewing a corn-based beer back in the early periods of their civilizations, circa 1200 A.D., 900 A.D., and 1400 A.D., respectively. Drinking beer has indeed been an integral part of mankind's history. Ladies, don't you think it's time to partake in this age-old tradition?

Fun Facts

The strongest that any alcoholic beverage can be is 190 proof, or 97.5% alcohol. (At higher proof, the beverage actually begins to draw moisture from the air and self-dilutes.)

~

Tom Arnold, Sandra Bullock, Chevy Chase, Bill Cosby, and Bruce Willis are all former bartenders.

~

The shallow champagne glass originated with Marie Antoinette. It was first formed from wax molds made of her breasts.

~

The national anthem of the United States, the "Star-Spangled Banner," was written to the tune of a drinking song.

~

Winston Churchill's mother invented the Manhattan cocktail: whiskey and sweet Vermouth.

~

A leading wine merchant and investor named William Sokolin paid $519,750 for a bottle of 1787 vintage wine that supposedly had been owned by Thomas Jefferson. In 1989, the day he planned to auction it off at a New York City auction house, he accidentally knocked it over, breaking the bottle and spilling the precious contents on the floor.

Fun Fact

The Top 5 beer drinking countries (based on annual consumption per capita)

1. Czech Republic
2. Ireland
3. Germany
4. Luxembourg
5. Austria

According to *The Top Ten of Everything 2001*

HOW TO APPRECIATE BEER

Whenever we go into a bar, we instantly order a mixed drink. Maybe it's out of habit, but we think it's because somewhere along the way, women never learned to fully appreciate the taste of beer. While doing research, we learned that women generally have a more developed palate than men and are better at identifying tastes and aromas – so appreciating the taste of a good beer should be just our thing. Below are some tips for the novice beer drinker on how to appreciate a good beer:

Step 1 Beer is judged by three criteria: head, color, and clarity. Head is the white foam at the top of the glass. A good beer will develop its head quickly on its own, not just because it is splashed against the bottom of the glass. When you drink a beer, the head should leave little trails on the side of the glass. These trails indicate that the head is of a thick but light and fluffy consistency. The color of beer ranges from dark brown to light yellow and is indicative of the beer's heaviness. As a general rule, the darker the beer, the heavier the taste. Clarity indicates technique rather than quality. Some beers are cloudy while others are totally clear. Both the color and clarity of the beer are up to your personal preference.

Step 2 After looking at the beer, sample the aroma. Try and identify the hops, which smell herbal, spicy, or piney. Sometimes the malting can make it smell sweet. If it is a dark beer it may smell roasted, like coffee or chocolate.

Step 3 The best part: Drinking. Okay, ladies, head back and CHUG! Just kidding. Don't do that at all – you'll miss the flavor. For best results, let the liquid sit in your mouth for a second and really try to take in the flavor. Beer ranges from sweet to bitter to a balance between the two. The extra flavorings that develop a beer's taste are decided by its brewery. Little things such as the smell of your perfume or the taste of your lipstick can affect how the beer tastes, so always remember to take those things into consideration. One last note: Contrary to popular belief, beer does not taste best when it is ice cold, but instead is at its peak taste around 45-65 degrees.

Understand that enjoying beer can require time and practice. It is an acquired taste, so be experimental and try a variety of brands and types of beers before choosing your favorite. Once you do, you may never go back to fruity cocktails again.

THE BREWERY

Microbreweries are mini-beer producers, making under 15,000 barrels a year. There has been a recent trend of opening up microbrewery restaurants, and oftentimes these restaurants have samplers of specialty beer produced in-house. Some breweries offer guided tours that can contribute to your beer education. Microbreweries and the beers they produce offer a more individualistic flavor than the mega-brewery national giants.

Megabrewers, such as Anheuser-Busch, Budweiser, and Coors, are the big boys in the business. Many of these companies have been around for over a hundred years. Anheuser-Busch was established in 1852, Coors in 1873. These companies were some of the great innovators in the industry, introducing such advancements as beer pasteurization and refrigeration. While these mega-brewed beers are quite prevalent, they are often critiqued by beer connoisseurs for their "average" quality.

Fun Fact

**The Top 5 brands of imported
beer in the U.S.**

1. Corona Extra – imported from Mexico
2. Heineken – imported from Germany
3. LaBatt's – imported from Canada
4. Beck's – imported from Germany
5. Molsen Ice – imported from Canada

(Based on the number of imports in gallons.)
(According to *The Top Ten of Everything, 2001*.
Information obtained by the Beverage
Marketing Corporation)

SPIRITS

Chances are, after many fun nights out on the town, you're well aware of the drink of choice of each of your gal pals. This is certainly true for Sam and me. If I happen to be the first one to make it through the crowd, and I actually get the bartender's attention, I order Sam a gin and tonic and a vodka and soda for myself. As we learned a little more about the bar, however, we discovered quite a difference between various liquors. I prefer Ketel One and soda and Sam fancies Bombay Sapphire and tonic. You see, we learned that the quality of liquor is wide ranging. There is a big difference between top-shelf or call brands and rail drinks or well brands. If you walk into a bar and simply order a vodka tonic or a gin and juice, then the bartender will give you well-brand liquor, meaning it is the cheapest brand behind the bar. A call-brand, albeit more expensive, is often better tasting and gentler on your head and stomach. While you may pay more for "top-shelf" liquor, the higher price translates to higher quality, and a smoother, better tasting cocktail. Listed below are some facts about each type of liquor, as well as a few call brands to remember for your next night out.

VODKA

Vodka accounts for more than one out of every four bottles of distilled spirits consumed in the United States. Vodka is not supposed to have a distinct taste, therefore it can be made from a fermented blend of almost any carbohydrate-containing material. Traditionally, potatoes were used to make vodka in Russia, but today most vodka is corn based.

5 Call Brands of Vodka

Ketel One
Finlandia
Grey Goose
Stolichnaya
Absolut

TEQUILA

Tequila is one of the few spirits with increasing revenues in the United States. It is also the oldest distilled liquor in the U.S., dating back to the early 1500s. The margarita, the most popular drink made with tequila, is rumored to have been created by a Tijuana bartender. Legend has it the bartender invented the drink for his favorite customer who couldn't drink vodka or gin. The customer's name was Marjorie King and the bartender named the drink for her in Spanish: Margarita. Out of all the brands of tequila, Jose Cuervo accounts for almost half of the 5 million cases of tequila served every year.

5 Call Brands of Tequila

Jose Cuervo
Don Julio
El Tesoro
Don Felipe
Patron

BOURBON

Bourbon is a whiskey made from a mash containing between 51% and 79% corn. Always aged in wooden containers, whiskey is any of the distilled liquors made from a fermented mash of cereal grains including bourbon, scotch, and Irish, Canadian and United States whiskey.

5 Call Brands of Bourbon

Jack Daniels
Jim Beam
Southern Comfort
Maker's Mark
Evan Williams

SCOTCH

Scotch is either a single-malt or blended whiskey. It comes from five different regions within Scotland. "Single-malt"

whiskey is produced without the addition of grain whiskey, thus making it pure and unique. In order for a scotch to truly be considered a single-malt scotch, it must be made in only one distillery, it must be made exclusively from barley malt, and it must be made in Scotland. Most scotch connoisseurs argue that the best-tasting whiskies are the single malts. Macallan's 1946 is one of the most exotic bottles of scotch on the market and runs for about $2,500.

5 Call Brands of Scotch

Blends	Single Malt
Johnnie Walker Red and Black	Glenlivet
Cutty Sark	Glenfiddich
Ballantine's	Macallan
Famous Grouse	Balvanie
Chivas Regal	Rosewood

GIN

Every gin producer has their own recipe. Each one adds their own blend of botanical or flavoring agents so that their brand has a distinctive flavor. Yet there are specific types of gin. For example, "London Dry Gin" refers to a style of gin that was originally made in and around London, but now is produced elsewhere. As the name indicates, it's dry in flavor.

5 Call Brands of Gin

Bombay

Bombay Sapphire

Seagram's

Tanqueray

Beefeater

HOW TO MAKE THE PERFECT MARTINI

When guys are in the mood for something a little stiffer then a cold beer, martinis are a cool and sleek way to go. As noted by Sarah Jessica Parker and all the *Sex in the City* girls, the classiest drink is James Bond's very own favorite, and here's how to make one. . . .

Necessities
- Martini glass
- Vodka or gin (depending on your preference), refrigerated or otherwise kept very cold
- Dry vermouth
- Olives

Things to know before you start
It is imperative to have the martini glass. Come on, the goal is to look cool and sophisticated – and that just won't work if you're drinking a martini from a paper cup.

Speaking of cool and chic, martini and cigar lounges are a popular trend. They serve a wide assortment of delectable drinks, such as the chocolate martini or the cosmopolitan. To locate one of these hot spots, check your city's Web links. There are lots of variations on the original martini, but for our purposes, you can choose either a gin or vodka martini.

The lingo

Straight up: No ice

On the rocks: Alcohol poured over ice

Dirty: With olive juice

Shaken not stirred: Not only will you sound chic saying this, but it may even be better for your health. The shaking creates a healthy antioxidant for your body.

Directions

Step 1 Chill the glass. This can be done by putting the glass in the freezer for a bit or you can put ice and water in the glass and then pour them out when you're ready to make the drink.

Step 2 Put a drop or two of vermouth in the glass.

Step 3 Pour the vodka or gin until it reaches the top of the glass. It is your personal preference whether you would like it straight up or on the rocks.

Step 4 Spear three olives on a toothpick and drop them in the glass. If you like your martinis dirty, pour a little olive juice into the glass as well. Some people like to stuff their olives with blue cheese (our favorite) or, to spice things up a bit, some use jalapeno olives.

Step 5 Enjoy – but watch out, girls, these drinks are really strong. Behave yourselves!

SHOTS

Whether it's a celebration or just a crazy night out, shots can be a fun way to mark an occasion. Quick and delicious, here are a few examples of shots that we've found go down easy and get the job done.

A Few Shot Recipes

Lemon Drop

4 oz. Absolute Citron
1 oz. Galieno
A squeeze of fresh lemon
Shake well with ice. Strain into sugar-rimmed shot glass.

B-52

1 oz. Bailey's Irish Cream
1 oz. Kahlua
1 oz. Grand Marnier
Shake well with cracked ice. Strain into shot glass.

Kamikaze

1 oz. Vodka
¼ oz. Triple Sec
Dash of lime juice
Shake well with ice. Strain into shot glass.

Sex on the Beach

½ oz. Vodka
¼ oz. Melon Liqueur
¼ oz. Raspberry Liqueur
½ oz. Pineapple Juice
½ oz. Cranberry Juice
Shake well with cracked ice. Strain into shot glass.

Mind Eraser

1¼ oz. Vodka
¾ oz. Kahlua
1 oz. tonic water
Fill glass with ice. Add Vodka and Kahlua.
Top with tonic water. Drink through straw in one long sip.

While these shots may be perfect for us gals, to drink like a man, stronger shots are what the bartender ordered. Not too sweet and not quite as smooth, these bad boys definitely pack a punch you'll feel in a hurry! Here are some top guy shots. . . .

* Tequila – serve chilled. For festive fun, take this one with a lick of salt first, then the shot, followed by sucking on a lemon slice. Hence the saying, "Lick it, slam it, suck it!"
* Southern Comfort – serve chilled.
* Jaggermeister – serve chilled.
* Goldschlagger – serve chilled.
* Jack Daniels – serve chilled.

WINE

Finally, any female who is serious about her drinks should be knowledgeable about wine, perhaps the most sophisticated drink of all. For many it is a serious passion. If you aren't well versed in the world of wine you should at least learn some basics. The information could prove useful when on a date. If you are at a classy restaurant and the man at the table is about to order a glass, here are some tips that will impress him and convince him what a hip chick you are. From Merlots to Pinot Grigio, there is enough material on wine for an entire book, but here are a few of the essentials.

Wine can be divided into three general types: red, white, or sparkling. (We often refer to champagne as a type of wine while in truth it is a specific sparkling wine that comes from Champagne, a region in France. Incidentally, wines are often named after their place of origin.)

There are many different wine-producing regions throughout the world. In the United States, California is home to the wineries of Napa and Sonoma counties. Outside the U.S., well-known wines from

France come from Bordeaux or Burgundy. In Italy, wines from Tuscany are referred to as Chianti. Some others countries with well-known vineyards include South Africa, Chile, Australia, New Zealand, and Israel.

As you may already know, there are different types of wine for each occasion and mood. Wines are often served with food to compliment its flavor. For example, white wine is typically served with lighter dishes, such as fish or chicken, while red wine is usually served with heavier meals, such as red meat or hearty pasta dishes.

Different types of wine are made from different types of grapes. The following are a few of the most common wines:

Cabernet Sauvignon: A red wine that is often hearty and full flavored. Cabernet often comes from the Bordeaux region.

Chardonnay: A mild white wine. California is notorious for the quality of its Chardonnay grapes.

Merlot: A popular, light-bodied red wine.

Pinot Noir: The grapes used to make Pinot Noir often come from France's Burgundy region. They produce a rich and full-bodied red wine.

Zinfandel: Served as a red wine, it is noted for its spicy taste and its strong full flavor.

Typically every bottle of wine indicates the year it was harvested. Generally, the older a red wine is, the longer it has matured and thus the greater its quality. Conversely, most white wines do not require aging and are prime for drinking directly after purchasing.

BUYING WINE

Last Thanksgiving a friend of mine organized a wine taste test for her guests. She picked four bottles of wine in a variety of prices and covered the bottles in tin foil, numbering them 1-4. Everyone at the dinner table rated the wine. Her guests ranged from those who considered themselves wine connoisseurs to those who hardly drank wine at all. After all the wines had been sampled, it was decided that the cheapest of the four bottles was the crowd favorite. The moral of the story is that when it comes to price, don't feel compelled to order the most expensive wine.

Many factors can affect the price of a bottle of wine. A single bottle can range from a few dollars to several hundred dollars. Wine is priced differently for a variety of reasons. Some vineyards are known for producing better grapes and, therefore, better wine. Some methods of making wine are more costly than others and this obviously affects the bottle price. Lastly, price is determined by rating scales and expert evaluations. Those wines with superior qualities will cost more.

TASTING WINE

Wine tasting is an experience that allows all your senses to participate. When ordering wine at a restaurant, the waiter will bring the bottle to the table, open it, and present it to the person who ordered the bottle while noting the label. He will then fill the glass about one-third full to allow the customer to taste it. If you want to look like a professional taster, here's what to do. . . .

Step 1 Look at the wine. Do this by picking up the glass by its stem, so as not to hinder the color with your fingerprints or the heat of your hand. By looking at the wine from a variety of angles, you will be able to see its hue, intensity, and clarity. If you are an expert on wine, the color can tell you many things, from its character to what type of conditions the grapes were grown in. If only men were this easy to interpret!

Step 2 Next, you want to swirl the wine, again by the stem of the glass. After spinning it, you should let it rest and watch it seep down the sides of the glass. The trails left on the sides of the glass are referred to as the "legs" of the wine. The thicker the legs, the higher the percentage of alcohol contained in that wine.

Step 3 Stick your nose in the glass and take in the wine's aroma. This will reveal more about your selection, ranging from what type of wine it is to how it was fermented. It can even tell you the wine's age; younger wines smell fruity while older wines retain a deeper, more complex scent as they age.

Step 4 Now what you've been waiting for – the actual tasting. You don't want to take

too much into your mouth. Sip just enough to get the flavor and to allow you to swirl it around in your mouth to get the full effect. If you approve of the wine, indicate this to the waiter. The waiter will then proceed to serve the other guests at the table and return to fill last the glass of the person who tasted the wine. The waiter will leave the bottle on the table with the cork.

Step 5 If it's a red wine, let it breathe a few minutes and then enjoy!

GLASSWARE

As any woman knows, accessories are an integral part of any outfit. Well, the same holds true with drinking at the bar. For my 21st birthday, Sam gave me a beautiful set of martini glasses, along with a complete bartending kit. (I get more compliments on the glasses than the taste of the drinks every time I entertain!) It's important to serve drinks in their correct glass. Here's a short list to help you out. . . .

A martini glass You guessed it, these glasses are used to serve martinis. They have a standard stem and open in a v-shape.

A champagne flute This is used to serve sparkling wines or champagnes. It's a tall, thin glass attached to a stem that is useful for toasting because it keeps the liquid from splashing onto your dress. In addition, it reduces the wine's surface area and keeps the bubbles from dissipating.

A red wine glass This glass has a wide cup that allows for a larger surface area so that you can take in the aroma. Also, the way you grasp the glass affects the wine's temperature.

A white wine glass This glass has a smaller cup than a red wine glass and should be held at the stem in order for the wine to remain cold.

Snifter This glass generally has a wide cup, resembling the red wine glass, but it comes to a smaller opening. It is used for after-dinner drinks such as brandies or cognacs.

A shot glass This little glass is obviously used for shots. Its size ensures you only drink a small quantity of the potent liquids you put in it.

A rail glass This is a regular drinking glass which is often used to serve mixed drinks.

~

This chapter's many hints are sure to help you appreciate the bar just the way all of your male counterparts do. The most important thing to remember is to have fun, but don't drink past your limits. At the end of the night, we don't want you throwing punches, or even worse, throwing up. So, don't ever lose self-control and don't succumb to peer pressure. Drink if you want to, not when your friends want you to. Remember that the most respectable drinker is the one who knows when he or she has had enough.

P.S. If you wake up in the morning with a pounding head, we hate to tell you, but there is no cure for that headache except the old fashioned passage of time. (Generally an hour for each drink you consumed.) Hangovers can be the worst, so our advice is to drink a lot of water and remember that feeling the next time you put a cocktail to your lips!

OUTSIDE THE HOUSE

Jenn and I first met at summer camp. In the mountains of North Georgia, we were exposed to the joys of nature, hiking, roasting marshmallows around a campfire, scary ghost stories, and eerie nighttime noises. Despite our fear of bugs and snakes and our distaste for campfire stew, we had a great time, and since then have continued to camp and enjoy the outdoors. You can too, if you take the time to be prepared.

VOCABULARY

Gore-Tex: A durable, waterproof, breathable fabric often used in outdoor gear such as tents, sleeping bags, rain jackets, backpacks, and hiking boots.

Briquettes: Individual pieces of charcoal

Carabiner: A lightweight metal snap that is used in rock climbing and rappelling as a safety device to keep various things connected, such as ropes, the climber, and the belayer.

External Frame Backpacks: These were the first packs used by hikers. Their external frame is made with aluminum poles and these antiques remain popular today. Not only are they reasonable priced and easy to pack, they don't rest directly on your back – thus allowing for increased air circulation. Ideal for a long day hike or a short camping weekend.

Internal Frame Backpack: First introduced in the 1970s, these packs have supportive and adjustable internal frames that are surprisingly comfortable. Better suited for the serious camper.

SUGGESTED PACKING LIST FOR A CAMP-OUT

1. **Tent** Before hightailing it to the woods, be sure you have all the necessary stakes and covers.

2. **Sleeping bag** Make sure it is waterproof and warm enough for the expected climate.

3. **Backpack** Whether it is a pack with an internal or external frame, be sure it is packed in a balanced fashion, it's not too heavy, and it fits comfortably.

4. **Matches and/or a lighter** An absolute necessity if you plan on building a campfire.

5. **Raingear** No matter what the predicted forecast, you never know when a storm will roll in and catch you unaware.

6. **Water bottles** It's important to stay hydrated on a camping trip and, as all girls know, you can never drink too much water. Be sure to carry several containers of drinking water at all times.

7. **Flashlight** Bring along extra batteries just in case.

8. **Sunscreen** A minimum of SPF 15.

9. **Insect Repellent** Good choices are Deep Woods Off, Repel Deet Sportsman, or Sawyer Deet Composite.

10. **First Aid Kit** Be sure to include the following: scissors, tweezers, various bandages, medical tape, anti-bacterial ointment, aspirin, burn ointment, a snake bite kit, a thermometer, Calamine lotion, and iodine tablets (or a similar water purifying tablet).

11. **A compass** You don't want to spoil your trip by getting lost.

12. Last, but not least . . . be sure to tuck **a trail map** (if available) into your pack.

Perhaps the most critical thing to remember when going camping is to be safe. "Safety first" should be your motto. When on the trail, you can really only depend on your own survival skills if something goes wrong. Take every necessary precaution. Don't wander off trails, do get enough rest, drink plenty of safe, clean water, and make sure to follow all signs and warnings. Most importantly, enjoy the scenery and have fun!

CHOOSING A TENT

Tents come in a wide variety of sizes and styles. And as you might know, outdoor stores can not only be intimidating, but downright pricey. So before buying that perfect tent, keep in mind the following information:

According to www.rei.com, tents can be divided into two main categories: three-season tents and four-season tents. Three-season tents are used for general backpacking, whereas four-season tents are more appropriate for harsher conditions and mountaineering. Tents best suited for winter conditions have dome-shaped tops so that snow does not collect up there. So, one big consideration when choosing your tent is the time of year you will be traveling. As for sleeping capacity, tents usually indicate how many campers can fit in them comfortably, but remember to take the size of the people you are traveling with into consideration.

Make sure your tent is:

1. Lightweight – You never know where you will have to carry it.

2. Strong, durable and made with quality components – There is nothing worse than being stuck in the woods with a broken tent. Before every trip, check to make sure your tent is in good condition. If it is not waterproof, be sure it includes a raincover.

3. The right size – Not only does this mean it should sleep the right number of people, but it should also be large enough to house your packs . . . if need be.

4. Suitable for the toughest weather conditions – Always be prepared to encounter unexpected weather. Pick a dependable tent that is solid and sturdy, whatever the temperature conditions.

PICKING A CAMPGROUND

Now that you have your tent and gear, it's time to head to the great outdoors. Picking the perfect campsite can make or break your trip. This past summer, Jenn went westward on a month-long camping trip. On more than one occasion, the campground her group was supposed to be staying at was either mistakenly overbooked, or the sites were so close to one another that there was barely enough room to set up camp! After a long, hot day of hiking, this can definitely be an unwelcome surprise. Don't let this happen to you. Follow these tips:

First – Always make sure the campground you are headed to is open and has sites available. Ask about their accommodations. Do they have running water? Phones? Bathrooms? Well-marked trails?

Second – Be sure to arrive at your site at least two hours before sunset so that you can easily set up camp and start cooking while it is still light out.

Third – Find out what kind of wildlife roams the area so that you can take the proper precautions.

Fourth – Try not to choose a site too close to others. Not only will it ruin your time away from the city's hustle and bustle, chances are you'll disturb them, too.

Fifth – Once you have chosen a site, treat it with respect. Throw away all your garbage and leave the site as you found it, if not cleaner! Be a minimum-impact camper.

Once while we were camping with some of our high-school friends, a few of the guys were overly confident about leading the way to our campsite. They refused to let the girls have any say in reading the map, and a few minutes later we were completely disoriented, 100% lost. We had no clue which direction we should be heading in, and as the sun started to set, tensions rose. Eventually – and luckily – we stumbled onto the right path, but for a brief moment, we were in dire straits. If you find yourself turned around and lacking a compass, follow our 5-step improvisation plan.

Step 1 Put a stick in the ground leaning toward the sun, but in such a way that it does not cast a shadow.

Step 2 Wait 15 minutes until the stick casts a shadow.

Step 3 Draw a straight line perpendicular to the shadow line.

Step 4 You can now read your self-made compass. The stick marks your West point and the end of the shadow is the East!

Step 5 Continue on your journey and enjoy a night beneath the stars.

HOW TO AVOID BEARS

Both of us are terrified of bears, and when we are in bear territory, we have to muster up the courage not to sleep in the car! Bears love the scent of food. If they smell something enticing, they have no qualms about feeding off nearby campsites. If you don't want an uninvited visitor at your next picnic, follow these words of wisdom.

1. When entering bear territory, always listen to ranger advice and heed the signs. Also, don't go alone. There is safety in numbers.

2. Keep your food and any scented toiletries (toothpaste, deodorant, etc.) tightly sealed and never keep food in your tent. Most often, bears want nothing

to do with humans. They're simply enticed by the scent of food. In fact, in 1998, a record number 1300 bears broke into cars in Yosemite National Park. Don't needlessly lure a bear in your direction – keep your food in bear-resistant food containers.

3. Be aware of bear clues. Look for things like fresh tracks or droppings. If you see some, change direction.

4. When walking in the woods, try to wear a bell or something else that will make noise as you move so that animals know you are around.

5. If you do encounter a bear, do not make eye contact. Slowly back away from the bear so they can see you are not a threat. Whatever you do, DO NOT RUN!

6. If a bear does charge at you, don't try to be a hero. Drop to the ground, curl into the

Fun Fact

Top 3 largest national forests in the U.S.

Tongass National Forest
(Alaska)
This forest is almost 17 million acres and is larger than the state of West Virginia.

~

Chugach National Forest
(Alaska)
Chugach is about the same size as New Hampshire, measuring 5.8 million acres.

~

Toiyabe National Forest
(Nevada and California)
Toiyabe was recently combined with Humboldt National Forest. Covering over 3.5 million acres, it is the largest national forest in the continental United States.

Fun Fact

The world's 5 highest waterfalls

Angel Falls, 3281 feet
Carrao River, in the Guayana
Highlands of Venezuela

~

Tugela Falls, 3110 feet,
Tugela River, Natal, South Africa

~

Utigardfossen Falls, 2,625 feet,
Norway

~

Mongefossen Falls, 2,540 feet,
Monge River, Norway

~

Mtarazi Falls, 2500 feet,
Inyangombe River, Zimbabwe

Each one of these falls is taller than the Petronas Towers, the tallest buildings in the world. Located in Kuala Lumpur, Malaysia, and looming 1483 feet tall, the towers seem almost "tiny" in comparison to these massive falls. The Sear's Tower, at 1454 feet tall, ranks directly behind the Petronas Towers. A Chicago attraction, it too would appear miniscule in relation to the world's tallest falls.

(Information based on total drop. According to www.earthlink.net/~geoffcon/facts.htm and www.worldstallest.com/93.html)

fetal position, and play dead. Most likely the bear will lose interest in you and move on. (This tactic has also been known to work if you are being hit on at a bar.)

THE TOP 5 MOST POPULAR U.S. PARKS

(According to the 1999 National Park Services Records)

1. Great Smoky Mountains National Park

North Carolina and Tennessee
10,283,598 visitors in 1999

~

This park is known for its plant and animal resources as well as its reminders of the age-old Appalachian Mountain culture. Part of the park's beauty is the many waterfalls that stem off from nearly every stream. The Appalachian Trail runs for 70 miles along the top of the park's ridge, allowing visitors to journey down its rich cultural path.

2. Grand Canyon National Park
Arizona
4,575,124 visitors in 1999

≈

A must for all tourists! The Canyon's enormous expanse is unfathomable until you actually see it. The park itself contains tons of hiking and biking, as well as donkey rides down into the Canyon. Campgrounds and lodging are found throughout the massive park. Nature lovers and outdoor fanatics should take time to visit this worldly wonder.

3. Yosemite National Park
California
3,493,607 visitors in 1999

≈

When we lived in Berkeley for the summer, everyone we talked to about exploring the state said Yosemite was a must-see. Considered *the* park of all parks, Yosemite is known for its incredible wildlife, gorgeous lakes, and rivers. It offers hiking trails of all levels, boat rentals, and great campgrounds.

4. Olympic National Park
Washington
3,364,266 visitors in 1999

≈

This park is known as "three parks in one" because it offers visitors mountains, the Pacific Ocean coastline, and acres of rain forest. Eight of the plants and five of the animals found in the park are not found anywhere else in the world! To cap off the incredible features of this fine park, it offers glacier-capped peaks that rise 8,000 feet above sea level.

5. Yellowstone National Park
Montana, Wyoming, and Idaho
3,131,381 visitors in 1999

≈

This is the first and oldest national park in the world! Home to the notorious "Old Faithful" geyser, Yellowstone has more geysers and hot springs than anywhere else in the world.

HOW TO LIGHT A CHARCOAL GRILL

Whether you are in your neighborhood or the backcountry, there is nothing better than a tasty barbecue. A good backyard grilling session brings a smile to everyone's face. Here are some tips to make sure your barbecue is foolproof.

To begin, remove the rack upon which you will be cooking the food. Spread a single layer of charcoal across the bottom of the grill. There are several ways to light a grill. We will only discuss using lighter fluid, but we know that there are lots of creative techniques, such as making a "charcoal chimney" out of a can and a coat hanger or by filling a milk carton with briquettes.

1. Squirt the fluid over the charcoal so that all the briquettes are covered.

2. Stack the charcoal into a pyramid and then move the bottle of lighter fluid very far away from the grill.

3. Finally, light the bottom of the pile with a long match or lighter and allow the entire pyramid to burn. Wait 15 to 30 minutes and do not add more lighter fluid. Once the charcoal is covered with a light gray ash, it's ready.

4. Using tongs or other long utensils, push the coal back into a single layer at the bottom of the grill, replace the rack, and start cooking!

My mom, Sandra, is one of the best caterers in Atlanta. To be sure your barbecue is a smashing success, follow the recipe on the next page for her simple and delicious marinade. It's guaranteed to be the hit of your next party!

Sandra's Manly Marinade

2 Tbsp dijon mustard

½ cup brown sugar

1 cup canola oil

⅓ cup soy sauce

½ cup red wine vinegar

⅓ cup lemon juice

¼ cup Worcestershire sauce

1 Tbsp black pepper

2 garlic cloves

2 sliced onions

1 tsp fresh chopped parsley

Rub outside of meat with dijon mustard. Sliver garlic cloves, pierce meat, and poke garlic into meat. Slice onions into rings and place on bottom of container. Place meat on top of onions. Mix rest of ingredients together and pour over meat. Cover and marinate 2½ hours. Drain marinade. Prepare meat as desired and then sauté onions and serve on the side.

Whether you set up a tent in your backyard or hike into the backcountry for a five-night stay, spending time outdoors can be a rewarding experience. Not only is Mother Nature beautiful and vibrant, she is peaceful and quiet. So, pack your bags and escape the frantic pace of city life. Give it a try – you may fall in love with the wilderness!

Bottom-Line Disclaimer

Any lovely ladies embarking on a serious camping trip should of course consult a thoroughly detailed backpacker's guide or similar outdoor guidebook for complete information. We love to camp, but we're not pioneers. Be sure you are fully prepared with all the necessary information before trekking out on your big adventure.

ENTERTAINMENT

Men the world over are seriously addicted to various forms of entertainment. Often even the most persuasive of females can't change the way men spend their leisure time. For example, my father watches four movies each weekend. He has for years, and I'm confident he'll continue to do so into old age. He is always informed on which movies are good, which ones are bad, and which ones he thinks I will enjoy. Most guys, however, only prefer one type of flick and would rather die than sit through the latest Mel Gibson romance. If a movie isn't chock full of espionage, action, and at least one bikini-clad babe, then forget it. So here is our humble attempt to make sense of the guy mentality with regard to the world of entertainment.

GUY MOVIES

(In our experience, here are the top 5 "guy" movies and why men love them, based on an informal poll.)

1. Animal House

Directed by J. Landen.

Stars Jim Belushi as an out-of-hand fraternity house member. Due to their wild parties, terrible grades, and slovenly lifestyle, the frat continually comes close to losing their "Delta House" charter. Most quotable line: "Fat, drunk, and stupid is no way to go through life." — Dean Wormer

2. Caddyshack

Directed by Harold Ramis.

Stars Chevy Chase in a hilarious satire of life at a prestigious country club. It makes a mockery of the club's members, caddies, and wanna-be members. And let's not forget that silly, irksome gopher that's always causing havoc. Most quotable line: "On your deathbed, you will receive total consciousness. So I've got that going for me . . . which is nice." — Carl Spackler

3. Fletch

Directed by Michael Ritchie.

Stars Chevy Chase as Irwin M. Fletcher, an irreverent newspaper columnist and master of disguises who loves digging up the latest scoop. Memorable line: "Using the whole fist there, Doc?" — Fletch

4. The Natural

Directed by Barry Levinson

Stars Robert Redford as Roy Hobbs, an overaged baseball player who comes out of nowhere to lead his team to victory with his nearly divine talent. Memorable line: "When I walk down the street, people will say, 'There goes Roy Hobbs, the best there ever was, the best there ever will be.'"
— Roy Hobbs

5. The Godfather

Directed by Francis Ford Coppola.

Al Pacino stars in this classic film about

the rise and near-fall of the Corleones, a leading Sicilian Mafia family. Won Oscars for Best Picture, Best Actor (Marlon Brando) and Best Screenplay. Most quotable line: "I'm gonna make him an offer he can't refuse." — Don Corleone

Godfather Trivia

In 1998, The American Film Institute named it the third greatest movie of all time, second only to *Citizen Kane* and *Casablanca*.

≈

What were the first four words of the movie?
"I believe in America."
Spoken by Bonasera

≈

**What city were portions of
The Godfather filmed in?**
Taormina, Sicily

≈

Who was shot on the massage parlor table?
Moe Greene

MOVIES FOR THE GUY ATHLETE

Baseball
"Bull Durham" and "Field of Dreams"

Football
"Rudy," "The Longest Yard," and "North Dallas 40"

Basketball
"White Men Can't Jump" and "Hoosiers"

Hockey
"Slapshot" and "Miracle on Ice"

Boxing
"Rocky" and "Raging Bull"

Video Game Timeline

The year was 1985 and Sam and I were only 6 years old, but neither of us will ever forget the unveiling of Nintendo. It became our daily goal to save the princess with the help of Mario and Luigi, or to collect the most tools for Zelda. In fact, we only went to sleepovers if our friends had Nintendo – we didn't want to fall behind on our skills. After a few years, we slowly outgrew our video-game obsession, but our male counterparts never have. Here is a brief timeline of the video game world as we know it and what we can look forward to in the future.

1972 Magnavox came out with the first video game called *Odyssey 100*. They had been working on it since 1966.

1974 Atari's *Pong* came out with simple graphics and a simple concept: bounce a ball on a board so that it hits colored dots which then give you points. Children across America were addicted.

1976 Although slightly more complex, Coleco was the next level of video entertainment.

1985 Nintendo – The video craze took off, and within a few years almost every American household had some version of a video entertainment system.

1980s and **1990s** Sega Genesis, Playstation, Super Nintendo, and Nintendo 64 followed in the path of the games of the past. With titles such as *Madden Football* and *James Bond*, featuring ever-better visual effects, video games were once again the must-have electronic toys for the country's youth (and the young at heart).

2001 and beyond Sony's Playstation 2 is the current hit. Playstation 2 offers the ability to play DVDs as well as CDs, and enhances visual graphics like never before. Other systems to keep an eye out for are Sega Dreamcast, Microsoft X-Box, Nintendo Game Cube, and Game Boy Advance.

HOW TO PLAY BLACKJACK

Sam and I get a thrill out of gambling. There is a true adrenaline rush involved in sitting at a blackjack table – and an even bigger one if you're winning. It is a favorite pastime of many of our guy friends who love taking chances. There's a casino thirty minutes away from me at college, and every time Sam comes to visit we take a little road trip to win some big bucks (hopefully). Although she often has better luck than I do, we always have a great time and have learned to "play the odds" over the years. Sad but true, you can never beat the odds . . . but if you have a few bucks to spare, it is a fun way to spend a few hours!

Blackjack's main premise is to get your card total as close as possible to 21 without going over. You are playing against the dealer, so your card total has to be higher than his or hers. The trick is that your cards are all turned face up so that everyone knows your score, but one of the dealer's cards is turned down. Once you get your original two cards, it is your choice whether to hit (take another card) in order to get closer to 21 or to stay (keep the cards that you have). The dealer does not have a choice. If the dealer's total is 16 or below, he or she has to take another card and if it's 17 or over, he or she has to stay. When every player has had their chance to hit or stay, the dealer flips over his or her second card and everyone sees if they won or the house won. If you take a hit that raises your card total over 21, you automatically lose – regardless of the dealer's unrevealed card. When you are betting on your cards, there is usually a table minimum and maximum you are allowed to bet on each hand. All bets must be placed before the cards are dealt.

In order to play the odds, you always assume that the dealer's "hidden" card is a 10. For example, if the dealer has an 8 showing, you predict the final total to be 18. Therefore, if you have 13, you want to take a hit in order to beat the house. But, keep in mind that a total exceeding 21 is an automatic loss!

BILLIARDS

Growing up with a pool table in the basement seemed to attract many guys to my house! In high school, two of my good guy friends and I had a nightly "study group." This "study group" invariably resulted in a series of pool games and mini tourna-

ments. Thanks to their excellent coaching abilities, I learned the rules and techniques needed to hold my own at the pool table. As we all know, guys dig savvy billiard babes. Here are a few tips to turn you into a pool shark the next time you're around the eight ball.

There are many different games that can be played on a pool table, such as straight pool, snooker, ten ball, and eight ball, eight ball being the most popular. Eight ball is played with a white cue ball (the ball used to hit the others), solid colored balls numbered 1-8 and striped balls numbered 9-15. A player's objective is to hit the set of balls numbered 1-7 or 9-15 into the six pockets spaced evenly around the table. The game begins with the balls being placed in a triangle at one end of the table. One of the players "breaks" the triangle to start the game. The players then take turns hitting the balls until someone shoots one into a pocket. If the first ball shot into a pocket is solid, then the person that hit that ball is "solid" from that point on. His or her opponent is "striped." (And vice-versa.) Once a player (or team) hits all of their designated balls into the pockets, they have to "call" their final shot and hit the black eight ball into the "called" pocket. If they do this before their opponent, they win the game. If a player hits the eight ball into the pocket before hitting all of their other balls in, they automatically lose the game.

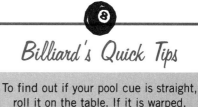

Billiard's Quick Tips

To find out if your pool cue is straight, roll it on the table. If it is warped, it will roll bumpily.

~

So that your stick doesn't slide off the balls, rub the chalk on the end of the table onto the tip of your stick.

Fun Fact

Recent male celebrities spotted playing pool

In New York Tom Cruise, Will Smith, and Paul McCartney

In Las Vegas Matt Damon and Ben Affleck

In London Brendan Fraser

GUY MUSIC

Everyone knows how influential the Beatles were. They revolutionized rock and roll and left a musical legacy that is still popular with today's youth forty years after it was recorded. Every guy knows all their lyrics and longs to have the same female following that John Lennon, Ringo Starr, Paul McCartney and George Harrison had in their prime. The Beatles' top selling singles were:

1. "Hey Jude"
Capitol Records, *The Beatles Again*, 1970

2. "Get Back"
Capitol Records, *Let It Be*, 1970

3. "Something"
Capitol Records, *Abbey Road*, 1969

Fun Fact

Top 5 male artists with the most platinum albums in the U.S.
(A platinum album is one that has sold over one million units.)

1. Garth Brooks, 97
2. Elvis Presley, 75
3. Billy Joel, 74
4. Elton John, 58
5. Michael Jackson, 53
   Bruce Springsteen, 53

(Ranked by number of units sold.)
According to *The Top Ten of Everything, 2001*

10 GREAT "GUY" ALBUMS GIRLS SHOULD BE ATTUNED TO

(Seeing that music is rather subjective, this list is based on an informal survey and the results are in no particular order.)

1. **U2** – "The Joshua Tree"
2. **Led Zeppelin**- "Led Zeppelin IV"
3. **The Rolling Stones** – "Sticky Fingers"
4. **The Doors** – "The Doors"
5. **The Beatles** – "Sgt. Pepper's Lonely Hearts Club"
6. **The Eagles** – "Hotel California"
7. **Pink Floyd** – "Dark Side of the Moon"
8. **Grateful Dead** – "American Beauty"
9. **Jimi Hendrix** – "Are You Experienced?"
10. **Nirvana** – "Nevermind"

THE SIMPSONS

When you ask guys of any age to list their favorite television shows, almost all of them will include *The Simpsons* in their top five. A clever and witty satire on

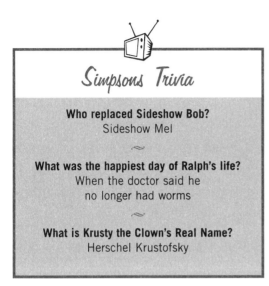

Simpsons Trivia

Who replaced Sideshow Bob?
Sideshow Mel

~

What was the happiest day of Ralph's life?
When the doctor said he
no longer had worms

~

What is Krusty the Clown's Real Name?
Herschel Krustofsky

American culture, *The Simpsons* offers laughs and dysfunctional scenarios that every family can relate to. After debuting in December 1989 with their "Christmas Special: Simpsons roasting on an Open Fire," this animated family has taken America by storm and changed the way many TV viewers think about cartoons. In fact, after more than a decade of air time, it's now the longest-running animated prime-time show.

Some famous names who have appeared on *The Simpsons* include:

- Aerosmith
- Barry White
- Gary Coleman
- Johnny Carson
- Stephen Hawking

THE WIT AND WISDOM OF HOMER J. SIMPSON

Classic Homerisms

- "I want to share something with you – the three sentences that will get you through life. Number one, 'Cover for me.' Number two, 'Oh, good idea, Boss.' Number three, 'It was like that when I got here.'"

- "Step aside, everyone! Sensitive love letters are my specialty. 'Dear Baby, Welcome to Dumpsville. Population: you.'"

❀ "Lisa, if you don't like your job, you don't strike. You just go in every day and do it really half-assed. That's the American way."

❀ "To alcohol! The cause of – and solution to – all of life's problems."

❀ "Don't let Krusty's death get you down, boy. People die all the time. Just like that. Why, you could wake up dead tomorrow. Well, good night."

Toss around some of this classic *Simpsons* trivia and you'll sound like a pop-culture expert. The next time your boyfriend agrees to cuddle up and watch your soap opera, you can return the favor by enjoying the next episode of his favorite show.

Conclusion

Well, there you have it! We hope you now feel better prepared to go out there and face "a guy's world." Be it a car or the bar, a little mouse in your new house, a sporting event or pitching a tent, you now have some answers to the questions that have plagued women for decades.

The truth of the matter is that this is not a book to make you manly – it's a book to let you know that, as a woman, you can do anything and everything you put your mind to. It was our intention to guide you through some common obstacles you may encounter, and to make sure you can complete some basic tasks without asking for a man's help. Take confidence in your own abilities. Ladies, we can't answer all your questions, but with this tutorial we hope we have given you a valuable foundation. Stow it in your car, skim it before your next date, or keep it handy on your coffee table for easy reference.

However, there are still some baffling questions about guys that remain unanswered. Why do grown men play video games like children? Why do they fail to ask for directions? Why do they think they are always right? The answers to those age-old dilemmas will give us plenty to write about in our next book . . . in the meantime, good luck!

Love,

Jenn and Sam

Sources

BOOKS

Ash, Russell. *The Top Ten of Everything, 2001*. DK Publishing: New York, NY, 2000.

Footman, Tim. *Guinness Book of World Records*. Bantam: New York, NY, 2001.

James, Sara. *InStyle Magazine*: "Stick Shift." February 2001, p.158.

Johnson, Anna. *Three Black Skirts*. Workman Publishing: New York, NY, 2000.

McCutcheon, Mark. *Descriptionary*. Checkmark Books: New York, NY, 1992.

Roberts, Jason. *The Learn2Guide*. Villard: New York, NY, 1999.

Sclar, Deanna. *Buying a Car for Dummies*. IDG Books World Wide: New York, NY, 1998.

Selwitz, Laurie. *Men are from Locker Rooms, Women are from Luxury Boxes*. Zumedia: Los Angeles, CA, 1998.

Schwab, Howie. *ESPN Did You Know?*. Hyperion/ESPN Books: New York, NY, 1998.

Shepardson, David. *Dietary Guidelines for Americans*. Department of Health and Human Services and Department of Agriculture: 1992.

WEB SITES

www.absolutetrivia.com
www.alabev.com
www.anheuserbusch.com
www.learn2.com
www.beerhunter.com
www.dailyglobe.com/beer/styles.html
www.drinks.txt
www.epicurious.com
www.ESPN.com
www.gameworld.com
www.golfonline.com
www.golf-historian.uk.co
www.housenet.com
www.infoplease.com
www.madd.org
www.nba.com
www.nfl.com
www.nfs.com
www.pga.com
www.rei.com
www.thesimpsons.com
www.uselessknowledge.com
www.web3.foxinternet.net
www.winespectator.com.
www.winespectator.com
www.worldstallest.com
www.earthlink.net

Acknowledgments

To Scott Bard, Tysie Whitman, Ann Lovett, Burtch Hunter, and everyone else at Longstreet who thought this was a good idea and helped us along the way.

To Samantha Davenport, Brett Schindler, Holly Peyer, and Chris Bingaman – who helped us a great deal with the book's layout.

To Arie Goldman – who did a fabulous job with photography for the book.

To our girlfriends who knew more of this stuff than we did before we got started and have encouraged us all the way – Rachel, Marissa, Hollie, Andrea, Mara, Amanda, Courtney, Susan, Gina, Robyn and Cori.

To those guys who attended our focus group, answered our questions, offered suggestions, or just bugged us enough about being girls that we felt compelled to write this book – Kevin, Jimmy, Wes, Adam, Jay, Brett M., Parker, Brett P., Gary, Patrick S., Patrick W., Greg, Dion, and Dan.

To Ezra – for support, extensive editing, and love.

To Kimberly and Richard – the most helpful and supportive stepparents around.

To Virginia and Milton and Naomi and Freda – for being supportive, encouraging, and caring grandparents.

To Garrett, Lauren, and Michelle – for being a part of our very first presentation and for liking our idea from the start.

To Betsy and Josh – our real saviors when we find ourselves in sticky situations.

To our dads Clive and Joel – for supporting us in our every dream and goal.

And to our moms Sandra and Barbara – for showing us how empowered, respected, and incredible women can be.